squeezed

squeezed

250 juices, smoothies + spritzers

Jane Lawson

Photography by Tim Robinson
Styling by Marcus Hay

LAUREL
GLEN

San Diego, California

Laurel Glen Publishing
An imprint of the Advantage Publishers Group
5880 Oberlin Drive, San Diego, CA 92121-4794
www.laurelglenbooks.com

All notations of errors or omissions should be addressed to Laurel Glen Publishing, Editorial Department, at the above address. All other correspondence (author inquiries, permissions, and rights) concerning the content of this book should be addressed to Murdoch Books® a division of Murdoch Magazines Pty Ltd, Pier 8/9, 23 Hickson Road, Millers Point NSW 2000, Australia.

NOTE: Those who might be at risk from the effects of salmonella poisoning (the elderly, pregnant women, young children, and those with a compromised immune system) should consult their physician before trying recipes made with raw eggs.

ISBN 1-59223-273-6
Library of Congress Cataloging-in-Publication Data available upon request.

Chief Executive: Juliet Rogers
Publisher: Kay Scarlett
Concept and art direction: Marylouise Brammer
Project manager and introduction text: Margaret Malone
Photographer: Tim Robinson
Creative consultant and stylist: Marcus Hay
Recipes by: Jane Lawson and the Murdoch Books Test Kitchen
Recipe introductions by: Francesca Newby
Text editor: Justine Harding
Food preparation: Wendy Quisumbing
Editorial Director: Diana Hill
Production: Monika Vidovic
Stylist's assistants: Tamara Boon and Ashisha Cunningham

Printed in China by Toppan Printing
1 2 3 4 5 08 07 06 05 04

The Publisher and stylist would like to thank Breville Pty Ltd for loaning superb equipment for use and for photography. They can be found at www.breville.com.au. Thanks also to the following companies for supplying furniture, props, and kitchenware: David Edmonds, Design Mode International, Dinosaur Designs, Jurass, Mitchell & Helen English, Mix (d), Mud Australia, Orson & Blake, (Napery) Sara DeNardi for Feast, Top 3 by Design, and Wheel & Barrow. Special thanks go to the following companies: Chee Soon & Fitzgerald, Cloth, and Signature Prints for fabric and wallpaper backgrounds; Pazotti Tiles and Bisanna Tiles for tiled backgrounds; paint for backgrounds supplied by Porter's Paints; Jonathan Ingram at InDestudio for custom-made cabinets; Flying Standard for models' clothing; ECC Lighting & Living, FY2K, Spence and Lyda, and Orson & Blake for furniture. Finally, warm thanks to our models: Tamara, Tasman, Brandon and Kaitlin.

contents

squeeze it   When life has run you ragged, and even when it hasn't, there is a place close by where help can be found. Let the kitchen be more than just a nod to necessary sustenance—make it shine with

some mighty fine juice concoctions. All you need are some fresh fruit and vegetables, a juicer or blender, and a little inspiration, and you'll soon have a whole lot of healing going on.

squeeze it

Many people make fresh juices at home as a way to look after their health. And with very good reason—a glass of fresh fruit or vegetable juice is an excellent way to get a little nutrition into one's system. Fresh juices can repair, protect, energize, and improve—not just the body, but the mind and spirit as well. These are serious benefits. Other people make their own juices simply because they taste good. This is also very valid: juices are delicious. As well, they are convenient, cheap, and easy to make. Anyone can make them without fancy equipment or culinary skills.

But more than health, more than nutritional balance, more than even the time-saving benefits of a cleansing breakfast in a glass, the reason people *really* squeeze, juice, and blend every day across the nation is because we're all budding scientists and artists at heart. Juicing allows us to bring our own creative interpretation to nature's bounty, to bring some order to the chaos of the fruit bowl and a little sense to the vegetables. Juicing lets us take A + B and make C. What's more, there's lots of noise, and things splash about, and different sizes and shapes go in and liquid comes out, and it may be slushy or smooth or frothy and thick, and sometimes it's sunset pink but other times deep crimson or vivid green—and we're the ones controlling the whole thing. Miraculous!

There are few times in life when you can give such free rein to your inner artist and feel safe in the knowledge that the results will rarely be less than excellent or beneficial. What could be better?

the good juice

The health benefits associated with regularly drinking fresh fruit and vegetable juices are many and of long standing. We're not talking about some newfangled fad here. But, equally, there's no time better than the present to repeat them. Juices provide energy to the energy-deficient, protect the immune system, have cleansing and settling properties, give encouragement to a flagging libido, and even make it a bit easier to get going in the morning. Fresh fruits and vegetables contain an amazing array of vitamins, minerals, and other trace elements that are known to be essential for good health, and digesting them in liquid form is one of the best ways to help them on their beneficial way. No commercially prepared juice is going to have the same fresh goodness as your own drink will. The following is a taste of the good things juices contain:

Antioxidants are powerful substances that neutralize potentially harmful molecules in the body. These molecules, known as free radicals, are normal by-products of metabolism, but stress, smoking, and pollution can boost their numbers. If left unchecked, free radicals may play a role in the onset of heart disease, osteoporosis, and cancer. Some key antioxidants are vitamin E (wheat germ, spinach, avocados), vitamin C (citrus and tropical fruits, green vegetables, berries), and beta-carotene (apricots, dark leafy greens, mangoes, tomatoes, watercress).

The body can't make minerals but it sure does need them. They are present in the body in small amounts and are essential for numerous jobs ranging from regulating blood pressure to keeping teeth strong and healthy. All of the seven major minerals and nine of the various trace elements are vital to good health. Found in rich supply in fresh juices are minerals such as calcium (dairy, figs, and fortified soy products), iron (dried apricots, green leafy vegetables, spinach, nuts), magnesium (nuts, especially almonds), potassium (bananas, dried fruits, tea), and zinc (eggs).

Phytochemicals are compounds found naturally in plants. They do not have a nutritional value but are thought to be needed by the body for disease prevention. "Thought to be" because they're secretive little critters, but ongoing research suggests that phytochemicals can lower the risk of osteoporosis, cancer, and inflammatory disorders. The only way to guarantee you get enough phytochemicals is by eating and drinking a wide variety of different-colored fruits and vegetables of the best possible quality.

You may well ask what do vitamins not do: they are vital to fundamental processes (growth, reproduction, tissue repair), are essential for the normal functioning of every organ in the body, and are needed to release energy from dietary carbohydrates, fats, proteins, and alcohol. Like minerals, most vitamins cannot be made in the body, and so must be supplied by the diet. Found in good amounts in fruits and vegetables are the B vitamins (bananas, dried fruits, soy products, wheat germ), vitamin C (citrus fruits, green vegetables, berries, tomatoes, some tropical fruits), and vitamin E (wheat germ, spinach, avocados, nuts).

Who would have thought that fruits and vegetables were so well equipped to fight the good fight? But they are, and so much the better for us.

the juice on juicers

Most juices and smoothies are made with one of two pieces of equipment—a juicer or a blender. Some recipes require both; others also involve the use of a citrus press. But that's about it.

There is no question that the best juicers are expensive and, for most of us, the hardest part about making fresh juices at home is the initial decision to buy the thing—and figuring out where to put it. When choosing a juicer, prices and reliability pretty much go hand in hand upward, but here are a few things to consider before you buy: Does the juicer have parts that are dishwasher-safe? What is the motor's size? How easy will it be to clean? How wide is the chute (will it be able to cope with whole fruits and vegetables)? Does it have low and high speeds? Is there a slide-in froth separator (which is about as

good as it gets)? The more expensive juicers generally do work better and last longer. They also extract more juice per fruit, so you get more for your money.
Juicers work by a process of centrifugal motion, spinning the fruit or vegetable pieces in a filter basket fitted with a rotating cutting disk, thus separating the juice from the pulp. The juice comes out the spout; the leftover pulp goes into its own disposal container. A few things to remember: always use the plunger to push food down the chute, not your fingers; use the plunger slowly (this will ensure the greatest amount of juice is extracted from the pulp, and will ease the strain on the filter basket and motor); and put the juice jug or a glass under the spout before turning on. If you wish, line the pulp-collecting container with a plastic bag, as that can be easily discarded later. Do

not let the pulp-collecting container overfill. Fruit and vegetables with a high water content, like tomatoes and watermelon, should be juiced on the slower speed (if your machine has this option); hard ingredients such as carrots, apples, beets, and fennel work best on a higher speed. All juicers need cleaning. Sad but true. A few tips: make sure the stainless-steel filter is thoroughly clean before use. This means cleaning it properly immediately *after* each use. Once pulp dries on the filter, it will clog the pores and is hard to remove. Watch fingers when cleaning the filter basket. Some juicers come with a special brush for washing the basket—use it. It will help.

As their name suggests, blenders mix and whizz ingredients to a smooth consistency. Look for those that can cope with crushed ice cubes. Capacity

varies, but the best are the stand-alone ones, as they produce smoother drinks. But, really, any blender will do. Chop ingredients such as orchard fruits and bananas finely for best results. Blending ingredients such as plums will give drinks flecked with the skin.

The citrus press is an old stalwart. Be it a simple plastic job, a wooden reamer, or a top-of-the-range chrome citrus press with handle, the process is pretty much the same. Take citrus, cut in half, place against citrus press, and squeeze and twist. Strain the juice of pits before drinking or combining with another juice. Always reliable, a citrus press is time efficient and easy to clean. If you don't have a citrus press, however, just peel the fruit (leaving as much white pith as possible), chop into chunks, and pass through a juicer or blender.

getting a grip

There is not much that can really go wrong when you squeeze, blend, and whizz your own juices. But there are a few ways to guarantee great drinks every time. Always use good-quality ingredients—there is nothing to mask their flavors, after all. Use organic where possible, and refrain from using ingredients until they are fully ripe. Use fruits and vegetables straight from the refrigerator so that the end result is perfectly chilled. If you freeze fruit, such as berries, cherries, chopped mango, and overripe banana, use the fruit within two weeks. After that, the flavor fades. Unless otherwise stated, juice fruit and vegetables with the skin on. Remove all pits before juicing. The seeds can stay if juicing but remove if blending. Wash produce before use, scrubbing tough-skinned varieties with a soft brush. Chop ingredients only when you are ready to chuck the pieces into the juicer or blender; otherwise you will cause unnecessary vitamin loss. Don't be shy—experiment, embellish, revise, or adapt recipes to find your preferred flavor combinations. It's part of the fun. Adjust the consistency of drinks by adding water or still mineral water for a thinner drink, or frozen fruit, crushed ice, or frozen yogurt for a thicker one. Sweeten juices by adding a dash of honey, maple syrup, or some ripe banana (though this will affect the drink's consistency). If adding sugar, always use superfine sugar, as it dissolves easily. Experimentation will reveal if you like drinks rich and heavy with ingredients such as bananas, or clean and sharp with flavors like citrus and ginger. On the whole, fruit and veg don't mix. Of course, now that you've read that, the first recipe you see will be a **fruit and veg combo**. Give it a go. When juicing fresh herbs or small quantities of ingredients such as a piece of ginger or alfalfa sprouts, bunch them together or send them through the juicer alternating with a main ingredient. Whole ice cubes can be added to the blender, but crushing them first gives a better result. There is also **something therapeutic** about smashing dishtowel-wrapped ice cubes against the kitchen counter or hitting them with a rolling pin. It's all part of the fun. Finally, drink juices immediately. If you wait, things start separating, colors change, nutritional value fades, and the flavor goes all wrong. This is especially true of juices containing apples and pears, which oxidize quickly. There is no time like the present with fresh juices.

berries 'n' cherries Berries (and cherries and grapes), what words can describe thee? Bold, bright, bounteous (for some of the year), brazen yet blessed, beautiful, beneficial, bodacious, and so berry berry beloved. (Little bundles of bursting brilliancy.) Such are these small, juicy fruits, appearing in their best purples and reds every spring and summer. Behold the berry! (And cherries and grapes.) Get into them.

Plump blackberries have a sweet, juicy flavor all their own and are best used within two days of purchasing or frozen for later use. Black currants bring a tartness that isn't suggested by their size. They are generally used in juice form, often mixed with other fruit juices. Sweet blueberries appear in late spring and are also available frozen. Little powerhouses, they are a fantastic source of antioxidants. Choose firm, plump berries and use within one week of buying. Cherries need pitting before use. Use a cherry pitter or cut in half and remove the pit with your fingers. It's not that hard. Use fresh cherries within one week of buying, otherwise buy frozen, pitted cherries. Fresh cranberries are rare creatures—use dried cranberries or cranberry juice instead. Potassium-rich, naturally sweet grapes are excellent for balancing other, stronger flavors. They ripen quickly at room temperature so are best stored in the refrigerator. Wash well to remove any insecticide. Buy fully ripe raspberries on the day they are to be eaten and avoid washing them, or wash them just before using, and handle them as little as possible. What raspberries lack in juice they more than offer in intense color and flavor. Sieve the juice after blending, if you like. Freeze when in season and buy frozen, unsweetened ones when not. Choose strawberries that are plump, glossy, unbruised, and firm and store in the refrigerator for up to three days. Wash and hull just before using. Use in the juicer or blender.

It's sweet, it's rich, and it's full of what you need.

What's not to fall for?

blueberry crush

1 cup blueberries
3 cups apple and black currant juice
2 cups club soda
1 tablespoon superfine sugar
Ice cubes, to serve

Blend the blueberries, apple and black currant juice, club soda, and sugar in a blender until smooth. Serve over ice. Makes 4 medium glasses.

Note: To make a slushy, add the ice cubes, crushed, to the blender when mixing the other ingredients.

Guaranteed not to leave you standing alone.

blue moon

2 cups blueberries
6 small peaches, pits removed
3/4-inch piece ginger
Pinch ground cinnamon
Honey, to taste, optional
Ice cubes, to serve

31

Juice the blueberries, peaches, and ginger in a juicer. Stir in the cinnamon
and honey, if desired, and serve over ice. Makes 2 small glasses.

Mix cherries with berries for a sensory overload, and let the apples add a note of calm.

berries and cherries

1 cup blueberries
1 cup cherries, pitted
6 apples, stalks removed
Ice cubes, to serve

Juice the blueberries, cherries, and apples in a juicer. Stir to combine and serve over ice. Makes 2 medium glasses.

Put on the Barry White, slip into a long, cool stretch of black velvet, and get in the mood for some love.

black velvet

2 3/4 cups black seedless grapes
2 1/3 cups blackberries
2 cups cherries, pitted
Ice cubes, to serve

Juice the grapes, blackberries, and cherries in a juicer. Stir to combine and serve over ice. Makes 2 small glasses.

Note: This juice is very rich and sweet, so only a small amount is needed. You can top it off with club soda to make 4 tall glasses.

blue moon

Complex and sophisticated, the sweet fruit is mellowed by the deep bass notes of cold black tea.

cherry and berry punch

2 cups cherries, pitted
1^1/$_2$ cups blackberries
1^1/$_3$ cups blueberries
^{3}/$_4$ cup strawberries, hulled and halved
3 cups ginger ale
2 cups lemonade
1 cup cold black tea
Zest of 1 lemon, cut into long, thin strips
10 mint leaves, torn
Ice cubes, to serve

Put the cherries, blackberries, blueberries, strawberries, ginger ale, lemonade, tea, lemon zest, and mint into a pitcher. Cover the pitcher and chill for at least 3 hours. Add ice cubes to serve. Makes 10 small glasses.

Serve with sushi on a Friday night and say sayonara to the workweek.

cherry blossom slushy

3 large Nashi pears, stalks removed
1 1/2 cups frozen pitted cherries
8 to 10 ice cubes, crushed

Juice the Nashi pears in a juicer. Add the juice, frozen cherries, and ice cubes to a blender and process until smooth. Makes 2 medium glasses.

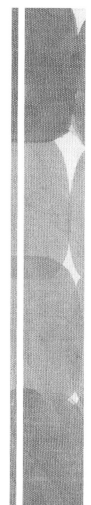

Life's a bowl of cherries, so juice them up and forget about the pits.

cherry, black grape, and apple juice

2 cups cherries, pitted
2³/4 cups black or green seedless grapes
6 apples, stalks removed
1 cup cranberry juice
Ice cubes, to serve

Juice the cherries, grapes, and apples in a juicer. Stir in the cranberry juice and serve over ice. Makes 2 large glasses.

Pour over vanilla ice cream for a sumptuous dessert.

cherry syrup

7 1/2 cups cherries, pitted
4 strips of lemon zest
Juice of 1 lemon
1 cup superfine sugar

Combine the cherries, lemon zest, lemon juice, sugar, and 2 cups water in a large saucepan. Bring to a boil and cook for 30 minutes, occasionally pressing on the cherries with a potato masher to release their juice. Strain through a fine sieve, pressing on the solids, then strain again into a very clean glass jar or bottle and seal. Refrigerate for up to 2 weeks. Makes 2 cups.

Note: To serve, pour a little syrup into a glass and top with club soda and a twist of lime. Also great in cocktails or in coconut milk with a dash of chocolate syrup over lots of ice. Delicious over ice cream, too.

cherry blossom slushy

Go ape for the grape and get some serious antioxidant action.

grape ape!

2 3/4 cups red grapes
10 apricots, pits removed
4 pears, stalks removed
3 apples, stalks removed

Juice the grapes, apricots, pears, and apples in a juicer. Stir to combine.
Makes 2 large glasses.

When the spirit is willing but the body a little sluggish, let naturally sweet grapes give you the boost you need.

red grape and cantaloupe juice

2 3/4 cups red seedless grapes
1 cantaloupe (or other orange-fleshed melon), peeled,
   seeded, and chopped
3/4-inch piece ginger

Juice the grapes, cantaloupe, and ginger in a juicer. Stir to combine. Makes 2 medium glasses.

Good things begin with g—gemstones, girls, and grape 'n' guava.

grape 'n' guava

2³/4 cups green or black seedless grapes
3/4-inch piece ginger
1 lime, peeled
4 large passion fruit
1¹/2 cups guava juice
Ice cubes, to serve

Juice the grapes, ginger, and lime in a juicer. Strain the passion fruit pulp well, discarding the seeds. Combine the passion fruit juice with the grape mixture and guava juice. Serve over ice cubes. Makes 2 medium glasses.

When you're melting under the summer sun, reverse the trend with this cool concoction.

zippy grape and apple juice

2³/4 cups green seedless grapes
6 apples, stalks removed
1 lemon, peeled
Ice cubes, to serve

Juice the grapes, apples, and lemon in a juicer. Stir to combine and serve over ice. Makes 2 medium glasses.

Note: Freeze the juice in ice-cube trays for a refreshing treat.

red grape and cantaloupe juice

Choose a sweet, mellow golden apple variety that will let the

raspberries shine.

raspapple freezie

6 apples, stalks removed, or 2 cups apple juice
2¹/₂ cups frozen raspberries

Juice the apples in a juicer. Blend the apple juice and frozen raspberries in
a blender until smooth. Makes 2 large glasses.

All work and no play is never a good idea—this drink helps factor in a little r 'n' r.

r 'n' r

2$\frac{1}{2}$ cups frozen raspberries
Juice of 1 lime
$\frac{1}{2}$ cantaloupe (or other orange-fleshed melon), peeled,
    seeded, and chopped
1 teaspoon honey

Blend the frozen raspberries with the lime juice in a blender in short bursts until the berries are starting to break up. Add a little water if necessary to help blend the berries. Add the cantaloupe and honey and blend until smooth. Makes 2 medium glasses.

Like a ruby-red stiletto, this is a sharp and sophisticated drop.

raspberry, pear, and grape juice

2 cups raspberries
4 pears, stalks removed
2 3/4 cups green grapes
Ice cubes, to serve

Juice the raspberries, pears, and grapes in a juicer. Stir to combine and serve over ice. Makes 2 large glasses.

The tart sweetness of Granny Smiths blends in perfect

harmony with the sweet richness of raspberries.

raspberry and apple juice

1¹/4 cups raspberries
6 Granny Smith apples, stalks removed
Ice cubes, to serve
Mint sprigs, to garnish

Juice the raspberries and apples in a juicer. Pour into a pitcher and chill.
Stir to combine and serve over ice, garnished with mint sprigs. Makes
2 medium glasses.

r 'n' r

Apple, berry, cherry . . . let's start at the very beginning, the very best place to start! It's an elementary choice, really.

abc

1¹/₄ cups raspberries
2 cups cherries, pitted
6 apples, stalks removed
Ice cubes, to serve

Juice the raspberries, cherries, and apples in a juicer. Stir to combine and serve over ice. Makes 2 large glasses.

This pink tonic is just the ticket for a lazy afternoon game of tennis with the guys.

raspberry lemonade

2¹/2 cups raspberries
1¹/4 cups sugar
2 cups lemon juice
Ice cubes, to serve
Mint leaves, to garnish

Blend the raspberries and sugar in a blender until smooth. Push the mixture through a strong sieve and discard the seeds. Add the lemon juice, mix well, and pour into a large pitcher. Stir in 6 cups water and chill well. Serve over ice, garnished with mint leaves. Makes 6 medium glasses.

This bird won't give you wings, but it will help ground your immune system.

strange bird

2³/4 cups strawberries, hulled
6 kiwifruit, peeled
Ice cubes, to serve

Juice the strawberries and kiwifruit in a juicer. Stir to combine and serve over ice. Makes 2 small glasses.

Ramp up the passion factor with a zinger of a juice—serve just before bed!

strawberry, cantaloupe, and passion fruit juice

2³/4 cups strawberries, hulled
1 small cantaloupe (or other orange-fleshed melon), peeled,
    seeded, and chopped
2 large passion fruit

Juice the strawberries and cantaloupe in a juicer. Stir in the passion fruit pulp. Makes 2 medium glasses.

strange bird

Haven't you heard? Rhubarb is the sweetest veg in town.

strawberry and rhubarb lemonade

2³/4 cups strawberries, hulled and halved
6¹/3 cups chopped rhubarb
1 cup superfine sugar
1 large mint sprig
¹/2 cup lemon juice
Ice cubes, to serve
Small mint sprigs, to garnish

Combine the strawberries, rhubarb, sugar, mint, and lemon juice in a large saucepan and add 6 cups water. Bring to a boil over high heat, then reduce to a simmer and cook for 15 minutes. Remove from the heat and allow to cool. Strain through a fine sieve, pressing on the solids. Strain again into a pitcher and chill well. Serve over ice with a small sprig of mint in a glass. Makes 4 medium glasses.

Note: Half-fill a glass with strawberry and rhubarb lemonade and top off with club soda for another refreshing drink.

Buff up for the beach with a nutrient-heavy detox draft.

summer detox

2 peaches
3 oranges, peeled
1½ cups strawberries, hulled
1²/₃ cups red seedless grapes

Cut a cross in the base of the peaches. Put them in a heatproof bowl and cover with boiling water. Leave for 1–2 minutes, then remove with a slotted spoon and plunge into cold water. Remove the skin and pits, and chop the flesh. Juice the oranges, strawberries, grapes, and peaches in a juicer. Stir to combine and serve with long spoons. Makes 2 medium glasses.

Let the season guide your footsteps—choose whatever fresh berries are available.

mixed berry and lemonade fizz

1/2 cup strawberries, hulled
1/3 cup blueberries
3 cups lemonade
2 scoops lemon sorbet

Blend the strawberries, blueberries, lemonade, and lemon sorbet in a blender until well combined. Pour into glasses and add any extra berries, if desired. Makes 4 small glasses.

A creamy cloud of fruity heaven, perfect for drifting along on a sunny afternoon.

strawberry, kiwifruit, and peach slushy

1^1/$_2$ cups strawberries, hulled
2 kiwifruit, peeled and chopped
1 cup canned peach slices in natural juice
3 scoops orange sorbet or gelato

63

Blend the strawberries, kiwifruit, undrained peaches, and sorbet or gelato
in a blender until smooth. Makes 2 large glasses.

mixed berry and lemonade fizz

orchard fruits   When apricots first came along, all things round, soft, and bottomlike sat up and took notice. When peaches came along, blossoms and downy creatures took heart, while pears gave

shape to artist's dreams, apples helped pies find their form, and plums

plumbed new depths. When things look glum, turn to orchard fruit.

It's hard to remain down when faced with a soft, round, yummy thing.

Apples are ideally suited to juicing and blending: they need only to be washed, their stalks removed, and then cut into rough chunks before tossing into the chosen machine. They leave little mess when used in a juicer and give a clear, cleansing drink. Avoid floury apples. Canned apples are good for blending. Velvety, ripe apricots are best used on the day of purchase. Remove the pits before juicing or blending. Canned apricots in natural juice and apricot nectar are both ideal for blending; dried apricots are suitable for infusions. Smooth-skinned nectarines are great in the juicer or blender. No need to peel but do remove the pit. The skin may fleck blended drinks. The same goes for peaches: juice or blend these babies. The height of summer is the time to indulge in peaches—this is when their flavor is at their fragrant, juicy best. Again, no need to peel, just remove the pit. Canned peaches can be blended. When juicing, pears need their stalks removed but everything else, cores and seeds, can stay. Peel and core when blending. Use pears that are just short of fully ripe—you want the natural sweetness that comes with ripening but with a little crunch to make juicing easier. Pear (and apple) juice discolors quickly, so add citrus juice and drink immediately. Nashi pears can be treated like apples. The best plums are pleasantly scented, yield slightly when pressed, and have a whitish bloom on the skin. Pit, then use in a juicer or blender. Prunes are dried plums—use them pitted.

Make this in the mellow months of autumn, when the orchards are heavy with sun-ripened fruit.

minted apple orchard

6 apples, stalks removed
3 pears, stalks removed
1 cup mint leaves, plus extra to garnish

Juice the apples, pears, and mint leaves in a juicer. Stir to combine and drink immediately. Garnish with a sprig of mint, if desired. Makes 2 large glasses.

Don't just grapple with a cold, tackle it to the ground with this vitamin-C–rich apple and zucchini drink.

zapple

6 apples, stalks removed
2 zucchini
1¼-inch piece ginger
Ice cubes, to serve

Juice the apples, zucchini, and ginger in a juicer. Stir to combine and serve over ice. Makes 2 large glasses.

Jazz up this gentle duo with a full-on blast of ginger spice.

apple, celery, and ginger juice

9 apples, stalks removed
9 celery stalks
1¼-inch piece ginger

Juice the apples, celery, and ginger in a juicer. Stir to combine. Makes
2 large glasses.

A shot of this green magic will get you through a gray day.

apple, celery, cucumber, and basil juice

9 apples, stalks removed
6 celery stalks
1 large cucumber
¼ cup basil leaves

Juice the apples, celery, cucumber, and basil in a juicer. Stir to combine.
Makes 2 large glasses.

minted apple orchard

No one can be sweet all the time—celebrate the sharper side of life.

apple and cranberry infusion

2²/₃ cups dried apple
1¹/₂ cups dried cranberries
Zest of 1 lemon
¹/₄ cup superfine sugar
Ice cubes, to serve
Fresh apple slices, to garnish

Combine the dried apple, dried cranberries, lemon zest, and sugar in a large saucepan and add 16 cups water. Stir over high heat until the sugar has dissolved. Bring to a boil, then reduce the heat and simmer for 35 minutes. Remove from the heat and allow to cool. Strain and chill well. Serve over ice, garnished with a thin slice of fresh apple. Makes 8 medium glasses.

Note: Serve the leftover strained fruit with ice cream or use it for a pie or pastry filling.

Revisit your cider-fueled student years without the grungy roommates tagging along for the ride.

apple fizz

6 apples, stalks removed
1 lemon, peeled
1 cup apple cider
Ice cubes, to serve

Juice the apples and lemon in a juicer. Stir in the apple cider and serve over ice. Makes 2 large glasses.

Juice in bulk and fill your best bowl—your guests will be pleased as punch.

apricot fruit spritzer

2 cups apricot nectar
1 cup apple juice
1 cup orange juice
2 cups club soda
8 ice cubes

Put the apricot nectar, apple juice, orange juice, club soda, and ice cubes in a large pitcher and stir to combine. Makes 4 medium glasses.

Everyone knows apricots look like cute little bottoms. They're also very good for you. Grab them while you can.

apricot, orange, and ginger juice

10 apricots, pits removed
6 oranges, peeled
1¼-inch piece ginger
Ice cubes, to serve

Juice the apricots, oranges, and ginger in a juicer. Stir to combine and serve over ice. Makes 2 large glasses.

apricot fruit spritzer

A sweet combination that's picture perfect for a couple of sweethearts to share.

nectarine, grape, and strawberry juice

6 nectarines, pits removed
2 3/4 cups green grapes
1 1/2 cups strawberries, hulled
Ice cubes, to serve

Juice the nectarines, grapes, and strawberries in a juicer. Stir to combine and serve over ice. Makes 2 large glasses.

Pungent basil leaves bring out the delicate sweetness of fresh
ripe nectarines.

nectarine and basil juice

4 nectarines, pits removed
1/2 cup basil leaves
4 oranges, peeled

Juice the nectarines, basil, and oranges in a juicer. Stir to combine. Makes
2 medium glasses.

Let exquisitely perfumed lychees clear out the cobwebs from a fuzzy morning head.

perfumed nectarine

6 large nectarines, pits removed
4 peaches, pits removed
1^1/$_3$ cups peeled and seeded lychees

Juice the nectarines, peaches, and lychees in a juicer. Save a thin slice of nectarine for garnishing, if desired. Stir to combine. Makes 2 large glasses.

Sit back and watch the world go by with a glass of this sweet, subtle nectar.

nectar of the gods

6 nectarines, pits removed
1/2 cup apple juice
1/2 teaspoon vanilla extract
1/2 teaspoon rose water
Ice cubes, to serve

Juice the nectarines in a juicer. Stir in the apple juice, vanilla, and rose water. Serve over ice. Makes 2 small glasses.

perfumed nectarine

The sweetest member of the rose family, peaches bring a flush

of unadulterated good health to the cheeks.

peach, kiwifruit, and apple juice

4 peaches, pits removed
6 kiwifruit, peeled
3 apples, stalks removed

Juice the peaches, kiwifruit, and apples in a juicer. Stir to combine. Makes
2 large glasses.

Like a Southern belle with a headache, this is a smooth number with bite.

spiky peach

8 peaches, pits removed
1 small pineapple, peeled
1/2 cup mint leaves
3/4-inch piece ginger

Juice the peaches, pineapple, mint, and ginger in a juicer. Stir to combine. Makes 2 large glasses.

89

Thick and smooth, this drink gives the mind and body a gentle nudge into the new day.

peach and cantaloupe juice

4 peaches
1/2 cantaloupe (or other orange-fleshed melon), peeled,
    seeded, and chopped
21/2 cups orange juice
12 ice cubes
1 tablespoon lime juice

Cut a small cross in the base of the peaches. Put them in a heatproof bowl and cover with boiling water. Leave for 1–2 minutes, then remove with a slotted spoon and plunge into cold water. Remove the skin and pit, and chop the flesh into bite-size pieces. Blend the peaches, cantaloupe, orange juice, and ice cubes in a blender until smooth. If the juice is too thick, add a little iced water. Stir in the lime juice. Makes 2 large glasses.

Add a little heat to sun-warmed peaches with a pinch of freshly grated nutmeg.

fuzzy peach

6 peaches, pits removed
1 lemon, peeled
Large pinch freshly grated nutmeg
1 cup ginger ale
Ice cubes, to serve

Juice the peaches and lemon in a juicer. Stir in the nutmeg and ginger ale.
Serve over ice. Makes 2 large glasses.

fuzzy peach

An apple a day keeps the doctor away . . . so double up and get ahead.

pear, apple, and ginger juice

3 pears, stalks removed
5 Granny Smith apples, stalks removed
1¼-inch piece ginger

Juice the pear, apple, and ginger in a juicer. Stir to combine. Makes 2 medium glasses.

This gorgeous juice is subtle and simple.

blushing nashi

6 Nashi pears, stalks removed
1 1/2 cups strawberries, hulled
1 1/4-inch piece ginger

Juice the pears, strawberries, and ginger in a juicer. Stir to combine. Makes 2 large glasses.

Note: Use pears that are just ripe but not overripe—otherwise they won't juice well.

Mint leaves plucked fresh from the plant are one of life's surest pick-me-ups.

pear and mint frappé

4 pears, peeled, cored, and chopped
2 teaspoons roughly chopped mint
3 teaspoons superfine sugar
10 ice cubes
Mint leaves, to garnish

Blend the pears, mint, and sugar in a blender until smooth. Add the ice cubes and blend until smooth. Serve garnished with the extra mint leaves. Makes 2 medium glasses.

Peppermint is well known as a stomach calmer and its fresh aroma can also lift your mood.

pear, melon, and peppermint juice

3 pears, stalks removed
1/2 small cantaloupe (or other orange-fleshed melon), peeled,
    seeded, and chopped
A few peppermint leaves
Ice cubes, to serve

Juice the pears, cantaloupe, and peppermint leaves in a juicer. Stir to combine and serve over ice. Makes 4 small glasses.

Note: The best way to select a ripe melon is to use your nose—if it has a strong, sweet fragrance and thick, raised netting, you can almost guarantee it is ready to eat.

pear, melon, and peppermint juice

If orange juice doesn't do it for you anymore, give this a go.

100   plum, orange, and vanilla

10 small plums, pits removed
6 oranges, peeled
1/2 teaspoon vanilla extract
Ice cubes, to serve

Juice the plums and oranges in a juicer. Stir in the vanilla and serve over ice. Makes 2 large glasses.

Note: Use the ripest plums you can find.

Some days you need calming drinks, other days you don't.

sweet and spicy plum

10 small plums, pits removed
1¼-inch piece ginger
1 cup cherries, pitted
3 oranges, peeled
1 cup mint leaves
1 teaspoon honey
Ice cubes, to serve

Juice the plums, ginger, cherries, oranges, and mint in a juicer. Stir in the honey, mix well, and serve over ice. Makes 2 medium glasses.

Yummy plummy in your tummy keeps you on the go.

plum and basil tango

10 small plums, pits removed
2 limes, peeled
1/3 cup basil leaves, plus extra for garnish
1 1/2 cups lemonade
Ice cubes, to serve

Juice the plums, limes, and basil leaves in a juicer. Stir in the lemonade.
Serve over ice, garnished with extra basil leaves. Makes 2 large glasses.

One of these once a week and it'll be once a day for you.

regulator

½ cup pitted prunes
Honey, to taste, optional
Ice cubes, to serve

Blend the prunes with 2 cups cold water in a blender until smooth. Stir in the honey, if desired. Strain and serve over ice. Makes 2 small glasses.

sweet and spicy plum

tropical-à-go-go Heady perfumes, sticky flesh, vibrant colors, and bizarre shapes are common occurrences among plant life in the world's torrid zones. For the poor witless juicer (meaning you and me), to meet

tropical fruit on their own terms is to enter into a strange world where

one mango is never enough, loved ones turn combatants over the last

passion fruit, and pith helmets seem entirely appropriate.

Blenders were probably designed with bananas in mind, even overripe ones. Just peel and chop and mix with yogurt, milk, or ice cream. Fragrant, slightly acidic, pink or red-fleshed, guavas have a short season, so they mostly grace the world already juiced. If you *are* using the fresh fruit, make sure it is fully ripe, then peel and dice. Small, green, and furry, kiwifruit are rich in vitamin C and potassium. Peel and dice for juicer and blender. For lovers of mangoes, no effort is too great—cut the flesh over the bowl or blender to catch the drips. Choose fruit that is heavy, with a sweet, rich scent. Some juicers don't mind melon skin, be it honeydew or orange-fleshed melon such as cantaloupe, but if in doubt cut the flesh away, deseed, and chop. The riper the fruit, the sweeter the juice. Only when a papaya is fully ripe should you seize the moment. Halve, remove the seeds, and scoop out the flesh. Retain the seeds if you want; they are edible. To seed or not to seed passion fruit? To avoid any grittiness, strain the pulp before blending. Papaya is yellow-skinned, sweet, and fragrant—ideal for the blender. A giant among juicing fruit, pineapple makes an excellent base ingredient. Chop finely and remove the eyes if blending. Choose one that feels heavy for its size and has a strong perfume. All parts of a watermelon are edible—remove the seeds if you like, or look for seedless varieties.

Get your motor running with this energy blast.

banana starter

2 bananas, chopped
2/3 cup frozen blueberries
1 red apple, cored
1¼ cups apple juice
2 ice cubes

Blend the banana, frozen blueberries, apple, apple juice, and ice cubes in a blender until smooth. Makes 4 small glasses.

Factor in eight scoops of sorbet—one for the blender, one for me, one for the blender . . .

banana, kiwifruit, and lemon frappé

2 bananas, chopped
3 kiwifruit, peeled and chopped
4 scoops lemon sorbet

Blend the banana, kiwifruit, and sorbet in a blender until smooth. Makes 2 medium glasses.

Drink your way to tropical heaven.

guava, pineapple, and pear

1 small pineapple, peeled
4 pears, stalks removed
1 cup guava juice
Ice cubes, to serve

Juice the pineapple and pears in a juicer. Stir in the guava juice and serve over ice. Makes 2 large glasses.

Note: For a smoother juice, cut out the woody heart of the pineapple.

Pale pink and lime green all of a sudden seem to go so well together.

guava juice and soda with zested lime blocks

Zest and juice of 2 limes
2 tablespoons lime juice cordial
2 cups club soda
3 cups guava juice

Put the lime juice, lime cordial, and half the club soda into a pitcher and mix together well. Pour into an ice-cube tray and top each cube with a little of the lime zest. Freeze until solid. Divide the ice cubes among 4 glasses and top with the combined guava juice and remaining club soda. Makes 4 medium glasses.

Note: The color of guava flesh will vary from pale yellow to soft pink. Look for the pink-fleshed varieties. They tend to be sweeter and have a slightly stronger fragrance.

banana, kiwifruit, and lemon frappé

Gorgeously green with a minty zing, this drink captures a fresh spring morning in a glass.

honeydew, pineapple, and mint juice

1 honeydew melon, peeled, seeded, and chopped
1 small pineapple, peeled
1/2 cup mint leaves

Juice the honeydew, pineapple, and mint leaves in a juicer. Stir to combine. Makes 2 large glasses.

Lacking passion with your honey? Just prepare this drink, serve, and look out.

honeydew melon and passion fruit

1 honeydew melon, peeled, seeded, and chopped
6 passion fruit (see Note)
Ice cubes, to serve

Juice the honeydew in a juicer. Stir in the passion fruit pulp and chill well. Stir to combine and serve with lots of ice. Makes 2 medium glasses.

Note: You will need about 4½ ounces passion fruit pulp, which will give approximately ½ cup of pulp. If the passion fruit are not particularly juicy, you may need to add some canned passion fruit pulp.

Cool down on a sultry afternoon with a long, deep sip of this chilled little number.

melon freezie

1/3 honeydew melon, peeled, seeded, and chopped
1/2 small cantaloupe (or other orange-fleshed melon), peeled,
    seeded, and chopped
12 ice cubes
2 cups orange juice

Blend the honeydew and cantaloupe in a blender for 1 minute or until smooth. Add the ice cubes and orange juice and blend for another 30 seconds. Transfer to a large, shallow, plastic dish and freeze for 3 hours. Return to the blender and blend quickly until smooth. Serve with straws and long spoons. Makes 4 medium glasses.

Note: Roughly break up the ice cubes first by placing them in a clean dishtowel and hitting on a hard surface.

Sweet as honey and soft as dew, you know this drink's just right for you.

honeydew punch

1/2 honeydew melon, peeled, seeded, and chopped
1 green apple, cored
2 oranges, peeled
Ice cubes, to serve

Juice the honeydew, apple, and orange in a juicer. Stir to combine and serve over ice. Makes 2 small glasses.

honeydew, pineapple, and mint juice

An excellent antioxidant, turn to this drink when you've been hitting the other grape juice a little too hard.

kiwifruit, grape, and orange juice

6 kiwifruit, peeled
2³/₄ cups green seedless grapes
3 oranges, peeled
1 large passion fruit

Juice the kiwifruit, grapes, and oranges in a juicer. Stir in the passion fruit pulp. Makes 2 large glasses.

The sweetest and gentlest of the melons, honeydew is the perfect companion to tart and tangy lemon juice.

kiwifruit, honeydew, and lemon juice

6 kiwifruit, peeled
1 honeydew melon, peeled, seeded, and chopped
1 lemon, peeled

123

Juice the kiwifruit, honeydew, and lemon in a juicer. Stir to combine.
Makes 2 medium glasses.

Serve this kiwi charmer to a new mom as a restorative tonic.

kiwifruit delight

3 kiwifruit, peeled and sliced
1/2 cup chopped pineapple
1 banana, chopped
1 cup tropical fruit juice
2 ice cubes

Blend the kiwifruit, pineapple, banana, fruit juice, and ice cubes in a blender until smooth. Makes 4 small glasses.

Some star appeal at breakfast and you'll be shining all day long.

star appeal

6 kiwifruit, peeled
4 star fruit (carambola)
1 small pineapple, peeled

Juice the kiwifruit, star fruit, and pineapple in a juicer. Stir to combine.
Makes 2 large glasses.

kiwifruit delight

Mango juice dribbling down hands and arms is part of the pleasure, but try and get it in the blender.

mango summer haze

2 mangoes, chopped
2 cups orange juice
¼ cup superfine sugar
2 cups sparkling mineral water
Ice cubes, to serve
Mango slices, to garnish, optional

Blend the chopped mango, orange juice, and sugar in a blender until smooth. Stir in the mineral water. Serve over ice and garnish with fresh mango slices, if desired. Makes 6 large glasses.

Mango has never had it so good—cosseted and surrounded by fizzy sweetness.

mango and mandarin chill

1 mango, sliced
2 cups mandarin juice
$1/2$ cup lime juice cordial
$1^{1}/_2$ cups club soda
2 tablespoons superfine sugar
Ice cubes, to serve

Freeze the mango for about 1 hour, or until semifrozen. Combine the mandarin juice, cordial, club soda, and sugar in a pitcher. Put the mango slices and some ice cubes into each glass, then pour in the juice mixture. Makes 2 medium glasses.

Note: For those with a sensitive sweet tooth, add the sugar to taste only at the end.

This thick juice will calm the storm of any upset tummy.

mango, apple, and lime

3 mangoes, peeled, pits removed
6 apples, stalks removed
2 limes, peeled
3/4-inch piece ginger
Honey, to taste, optional

Juice the mangoes, apples, limes, and ginger in a juicer. Stir in a little honey, if desired. Makes 2 medium glasses.

It takes two to tango, so try not to drink this on your own.

mango tango

2 mangoes, peeled, pits removed
1 small pineapple, peeled
2 large passion fruit
1¹/2 cups sparkling grape juice

Juice the mangoes and pineapple in a juicer. Stir in the passion fruit pulp and grape juice. Makes 2 large glasses.

mango summer haze

Sprinkle some orange nasturtium petals over the glasses and this drink becomes almost too pretty to drink. Almost.

papaya crush with lime sorbet

2 cups chopped red papaya
1 to 2 tablespoons lime juice
4 scoops lime sorbet
Crushed ice
Lime zest, to garnish

Blend the papaya, lime juice, 2 scoops of lime sorbet, and some crushed ice in a blender until thick and smooth. Pour into 2 tall glasses and top each with a scoop of sorbet. Garnish with lime zest and serve with spoons. Makes 2 large glasses.

For a sunrise special, juice the strawberries separately, then stir them through in a loose crimson swirl.

papaya, cantaloupe, and strawberry juice

1 papaya
1 cantaloupe (or other orange-fleshed melon), peeled,
    seeded, and chopped
2 3/4 cups strawberries, hulled
2 limes, peeled
Ice cubes, to serve

Juice the papaya, cantaloupe, strawberries, and limes in a juicer. Stir to combine and serve over ice. Makes 2 medium glasses.

Aloha summer, here we come.

hawaiian crush

2/3 cup chopped papaya
1 cup chopped watermelon
1 cup apple juice
6 large ice cubes

Blend the papaya, watermelon, apple juice, and ice cubes in a blender until smooth. Chill well. Makes 2 medium glasses.

Clean, crisp lychees hook up with earthy passion fruit for an affair worth remembering.

lychee passion fizz

2²/₃ cups peeled and seeded lychees
³/₄-inch piece ginger
3 large passion fruit
2 cups lemonade or club soda

Juice the lychees and ginger in a juicer. Stir in the passion fruit pulp and lemonade or club soda. Makes 2 large glasses.

hawaiian crush

Alive with intense flavors, this sweet syrup lifts fizzy water into the realm of the divine.

passion fruit syrup

6 large passion fruit
1/2 cup lemon juice
1/2 cup superfine sugar

Combine the passion fruit pulp, lemon juice, sugar, and 2 cups water in a saucepan over high heat. Stir until the sugar has dissolved. Bring to a boil, then reduce to a simmer and cook for 1 1/2 hours or until reduced by half and slightly syrupy. Allow to cool, then strain, pressing on the solids. Pour into a very clean glass jar or bottle and seal. Refrigerate for up to 2 weeks. Makes 1 1/2 cups.

Note: To serve, pour a little syrup into a glass with ice and top with club soda, lemonade, or ginger ale.

The wrinklier the passion fruit, the sweeter the pulp, so get down with an oldie.

passion fruit lime crush

6 large passion fruit
3/4 cup lime juice cordial
3 cups ginger ale
Crushed ice, to serve

Combine the passion fruit pulp, cordial, and ginger ale in a large pitcher and mix together well. Half-fill 4 large glasses with crushed ice and add the passion fruit mixture. Makes 4 large glasses.

If it's all been a bit of a blur so far, let this tangy tropical blend set you straight.

morning blended fruit juice

1/2 pineapple, peeled and chopped
1 large pear, stalk removed
1 banana, chopped
1/4 cup chopped papaya
1 1/2 cups orange juice

Blend the pineapple, pear, banana, papaya, and orange juice in a blender until smooth. Makes 4 medium glasses.

If you're feeling truly indulgent, serve this luscious juice over ice cream for a tropicana fantasy.

tropical fruit frappé

1 cup chopped pineapple
1/4 small cantaloupe (or other orange-fleshed melon), peeled,
    seeded, and chopped
1 banana, chopped
1 cup chopped papaya
1 mango, chopped
1 cup pineapple juice
Crushed ice

Blend the pineapple, cantaloupe, banana, papaya, and mango in a blender until smooth. Add the pineapple juice and crushed ice and blend until the frappé is thick and the ice has thoroughly broken down. Serves 4.

Note: This makes a great breakfast in a glass. The fruit must be ripe or you'll need to add sugar. Add a little coconut milk if you prefer a creamy drink.

passion fruit syrup

The mild green goodness of the kiwifruit gently undercuts the acid kick of the pineapple.

pineapple, kiwifruit, and mint

1/2 small pineapple, peeled
6 kiwifruit, peeled
1/2 cup mint leaves
3/4-inch piece ginger

Juice the pineapple, kiwifruit, mint, and ginger in a juicer. Stir to combine.
Makes 2 medium glasses.

This smooth, thick drink has style and substance—it can't help but be good for you.

tropical slurp

1 small pineapple, peeled
3 oranges, peeled
1 large banana, chopped
1 mango, chopped
Ice cubes, to serve

Juice the pineapple and oranges in a juicer. Transfer to a blender, add the banana and mango, and blend until smooth. Serve over ice. Makes 2 medium glasses.

Bewitch yourself with this tingly little number.

fresh pineapple juice with mandarin sorbet

1 large pineapple, peeled
1 cup ginger ale

4 scoops mandarin sorbet

Juice the pineapple in a juicer. Combine the pineapple juice and ginger ale in a large pitcher and chill. Stir to combine, pour into 2 glasses, and top each with 2 scoops of sorbet. Makes 2 medium glasses.

Sweet yet slightly astringent, this drink can catch you off guard.

pineapple delight

1/2 pineapple, peeled and chopped
2 cups lemonade
2 tablespoons lime juice
Mint leaves, to garnish

149

Blend the pineapple in a blender for 1–2 minutes, or until as smooth as possible. Pour the lemonade into a pitcher and stir in the pineapple purée. Add the lime juice and mix well. Serve garnished with mint leaves. Makes 4 small glasses.

fresh pineapple juice with mandarin sorbet

Sometimes only a bit of rough will do.

rough melon

4 cups chopped watermelon
1 small pineapple, peeled
2³/4 cups green seedless grapes

Juice the watermelon, pineapple, and grapes in a juicer. Stir to combine.
Makes 2 large glasses.

Open your eyes to the joy of a long, cool, liquid breakfast.

watermelon breakfast juice

3¹/2 cups chopped watermelon
2 tablespoons lime juice
¹/2- to ³/4-inch piece ginger, grated, to taste
2 tablespoons chopped mint

153

Blend the watermelon, lime juice, ginger, and mint in a blender in short bursts. (Be careful not to overblend or the mixture will go frothy.) Makes 2 large glasses.

Even endless summers drift to a close—help them linger with this slow, cool number.

watermelon and kiwifruit cooler

6 cups chopped watermelon
6 kiwifruit, peeled
Ice cubes, to serve

Juice the watermelon and kiwifruit in a juicer. Stir to combine and serve over ice. Makes 2 medium glasses.

This drink fixes you up all squeaky clean on the inside; shame it's not a toner, too.

watermelon and guava cleanser

4 cups chopped watermelon
1¼-inch piece ginger
⅓ cup mint leaves
2 cups guava juice
Ice cubes, to serve

Juice the watermelon, ginger, and mint in a juicer. Stir in the guava juice and serve over ice. Makes 2 large glasses.

watermelon breakfast juice

The ultimate thirst-quencher, watermelon makes a satisfying base for this piquant cooler.

watermelon, grape, and peach juice

4 cups chopped watermelon
2³/₄ cups green or red seedless grapes
4 peaches, pits removed
2 large passion fruit

Juice the watermelon, grapes, and peaches in a juicer. Stir in the passion fruit pulp. Makes 2 large glasses.

Been living on the wild side? Give your kidneys a chance to regroup with this healing drink.

kidney cleanser

4 cups chopped watermelon
1 large cucumber
3 apples, stalks removed
1 cup cranberry juice

Juice the watermelon, cucumber, and apples in a juicer. Stir in the cranberry juice. Makes 2 large glasses.

Think plump and juicy when choosing strawberries. Repeat out loud: plump and juicy.

watermelon and strawberry slushy

10 cups chopped watermelon (about 1 large watermelon)
1 1/2 cups strawberries, hulled
2 teaspoons superfine sugar

Combine the watermelon, strawberries, and sugar in a bowl. Save some watermelon for garnishing. Blend the mixture in batches in a blender until smooth, then pour into a shallow metal tray. Cover with plastic wrap and freeze for 2–3 hours, or until the mixture begins to freeze. Return to the blender and blend quickly to break up the ice. Cut the reserved watermelon into 6 small triangles and fix onto the edge of the glasses. Makes 6 medium glasses.

Create a thousand and one Arabian nights of your own with this petal-scented sparkler.

watermelon rose water slushy

3 cups chopped watermelon
1 teaspoon rose water
1 teaspoon lemon juice
2 cups lemonade

Blend the watermelon in a blender until smooth. Combine with the rose water, lemon juice, and lemonade, then pour into a shallow metal tray. Cover with plastic wrap and freeze for 2 hours, or until just solid around the edges. Return to the blender and blend until thick and slushy. Makes 4 large glasses.

Note: Watermelons are now available almost year-round but tend to be sweeter in the warmer months. Choose one that feels heavy for its size.

watermelon and strawberry slushy

citrus burst Short, sharp, tart, tangy, testy, zesty, mouth-puckering, muscle-clenching, jaw-clinching, eye-popping, shackle-shaking, thirst-quenching, stomach-clutching, sobriety-inducing, temper-tampering, sour-pussing, grizzly-gripping, gusto-making, constitution-shaking, mood-meddling, spine-tingling, total body-cleansing, fleet-of-footing, exhilarating, illuminating, and straight-talking citrus! Believe it or not.

The largest of the citrus, grapefruit packs a punch. Choose heavy fruit with unblemished skins. Pink and ruby varieties are sweeter and result in prettily colored juices. Grapefruit can be used in a juicer, with or without the peel (you get more pectin and antioxidants if the peel is added), in the blender, or halved and squeezed on a citrus press. A word of caution: if taking medication, consult your doctor before drinking large doses. The indispensable lemon has a dual purpose in juices. First, for flavor, and second, as a means of preventing fruit such as apples and pears from discoloring. Thin-skinned organic lemons can be juiced without peeling. Otherwise, peel thinly, leaving as much of the white pith as possible, then juice. As with lemons, limes can be used to prevent discoloration of fruits. The flavor also cuts through the richness of other fruits, particularly tropical ones. Roll limes on the countertop to get the most juice out of them. Use on a citrus press or peel and add to a juicer. Buy oranges that feel heavy and have tight skin. Use in a citrus press, juicer, or blender. Navel oranges are nearly always seedless, so they are a good choice. Blood oranges are sweeter and smaller than standard oranges and ensure a great color in drinks—grab them when in season. Mandarins (and other small citrus such as clementines and tangerines) are smaller and often a bit sweeter than oranges. Juicy clementines have a slight hint of acidity. They go well with warming flavors such as cinnamon and cloves in infused drinks.

Sweet yet light, this is the perfect juice for an unusually delicate morning.

grapefruit, pear, and guava

2 grapefruit, peeled
4 pears, stalks removed
1¹/₂ cups guava juice
Ice cubes, to serve

Juice the grapefruit and pears in a juicer. Stir in the guava juice and serve over ice. Makes 2 large glasses.

Pretty in pink with an acid twist—there's nothing sugary about
this tart cooler.

pink grapefruit, mint, and cranberry juice

2 pink grapefruit
2 cups cranberry juice
2 tablespoons finely chopped mint leaves
Ice cubes, to serve

Squeeze the juice from the grapefruit. Stir in the cranberry juice and mint
and serve over ice. Makes 2 large glasses.

Drink this baby and you'll soon be back in the pink.

think pink

3 pink grapefruit, peeled
1¹/2 cups strawberries, hulled
1¹/2 cups guava juice
Ice cubes, to serve

Juice the grapefruit and strawberries in a juicer. Stir in the guava juice and serve over ice. Makes 2 large glasses.

A froufrou fancy for a girly afternoon.

pink pom-pom

4 pink grapefruit, peeled
2 3/4 cups black seedless grapes
3 large passion fruit
1 teaspoon pomegranate syrup
Honey, to taste
Ice cubes, to serve

Juice the grapefruit and grapes in a juicer. Stir through the passion fruit pulp, pomegranate syrup, and honey and serve over ice. Makes 2 large glasses.

think pink

A delightful mix of tart and fizzy, serve in tulip champagne glasses as a light dessert.

ruby grapefruit and lemon sorbet fizz

2 cups ruby grapefruit juice
1 cup club soda
1 tablespoon superfine sugar
4 scoops lemon sorbet

Combine the grapefruit juice, club soda, and sugar in a pitcher and chill. Pour into 4 champagne glasses and top each with a scoop of sorbet. Makes 4 small glasses.

For a nightlife moment without the morning-after hangover, kick back with a sober mule.

sober mule

3 grapefruit, peeled
1/3 cup mint leaves
1 1/2 cups ginger ale
Ice cubes, to serve
2 small mint sprigs, to garnish

Juice the grapefruit and mint in a juicer. Stir in the ginger ale and serve over ice, garnished with small mint sprigs. Makes 2 large glasses.

Sometimes all you need is a big hug. If that's not available, this drink is the next best thing.

lemon soother

1/2 lemon, thinly sliced
1 large sprig lemon thyme
1 stem lemon grass, bruised
Honey, to taste, optional

Put the lemon, lemon thyme, and lemon grass in the base of a large, heatproof pitcher and pour in 4 cups boiling water. Set aside to infuse for 10–15 minutes. Serve hot or warm with some honey, if desired. Makes 4 medium glasses.

This refreshing, slightly tart drink is perfect for a picnic. Just blend with ice, fill a thermos, and enjoy the great outdoors.

lemon and green apple thirst quencher

¹/₃ cup lemon juice
6 green apples, stalks removed
Mint leaves, to garnish

Pour the lemon juice into a serving pitcher. Juice the apples in a juicer. Add the apple juice to the lemon juice and stir to combine. Serve garnished with mint leaves. Makes 2 medium glasses.

lemon soother

Beat Granny at her own game with this zesty lemon refresher—just make sure you save her a glass.

just-like-grandma-made lemonade

15 lemons
1$\frac{1}{2}$ cups sugar
Ice cubes, to serve
Lemon balm leaves, to serve
Lemon slices, to serve

Juice the lemons in a citrus press. Put the lemon juice and any pulp in a large nonmetallic bowl. Add the sugar and $\frac{1}{2}$ cup boiling water and stir until the sugar has dissolved. Add 6 cups water and stir well. Transfer to a large pitcher, add ice cubes, and float the lemon balm leaves and lemon slices on top. Makes 6 small glasses.

Running low on funds? Take a tip from childhood and set up a stall of your own.

homemade lemonade

2³/4 cups lemon juice
1¹/4 cups superfine sugar
Ice cubes, to serve
Mint leaves, to garnish

Combine the lemon juice and sugar in a large bowl and stir until the sugar has dissolved. Pour into a large pitcher. Add 5 cups water, stir well, and chill. Serve over ice, garnished with a few mint leaves. Makes 6 medium glasses.

Nutritious and soothing for the stomach, homemade lemon-barley water is the real thing.

lemon-barley water

½ cup pearl barley
3 lemons
½ cup superfine sugar
Crushed ice, to serve
Lemon slices, to garnish

Wash the barley well and put in a medium pan. Using a sharp vegetable peeler, remove the zest from the lemons, avoiding the bitter white pith. Juice the lemons in a citrus press. Add the lemon zest and 7 cups water to the barley and bring to a boil. Simmer for 30 minutes. Add the sugar and mix well to dissolve. Remove from the heat and set aside to cool. Strain the liquid into a pitcher and add the lemon juice. Serve over crushed ice, garnished with lemon slices. Makes 4 small glasses.

This sparkling little number will put a spring in your step.

lemon, lime, and soda with citrus ice cubes

1 lemon
1 lime
2¹/2 tablespoons lemon juice
²/3 cup lime juice cordial
2¹/2 cups club soda
Ice cubes, to serve

Using a sharp knife, remove the zest and white pith from the lemon and lime. Cut between the membranes to release the segments. Put a lemon and lime segment in each hole of an ice-cube tray and cover with water. Freeze for 2–3 hours, or until firm. Combine the lemon juice, lime juice cordial, and club soda. Pour into 2 glasses and add the ice cubes. Makes 2 medium glasses.

homemade lemonade

Turn up the heat!

lime and chili crush

6 limes, peeled
1 cup mint leaves
2 teaspoons superfine sugar
1/2 cup cold water
Ice cubes, to serve
1 chili, halved lengthwise and seeded

Juice the limes and mint in a juicer. Stir in the sugar and 1/2 cup water until the sugar has dissolved. Fill 2 medium glasses with ice and place half a chili in each. Pour in the juice and stir, pressing the chili gently with the back of a spoon to release some heat. Makes 2 medium glasses.

Get to know this kiwifruit sparkler and it could be the beginning of a beautiful friendship.

lime and kiwifruit sparkler

2 limes, peeled
9 kiwifruit, peeled
1 1/2 cups ginger ale
Mint sprigs, to garnish
Lime slices, to garnish
Ice cubes, to serve

Juice the limes and kiwifruit in a juicer. Stir in the ginger ale and serve over ice with a mint sprig and lime slices. Makes 2 large glasses.

Burst onto the scene with this feel-good golden blast.

pine lime and strawberry burst

1 pineapple, peeled
2 limes, peeled
2³/4 cups strawberries, hulled

Juice the pineapple, limes, and strawberries in a juicer. Stir to combine.
Makes 2 medium glasses.

Take the sting out of an early start with this citrus antidote.

citrus sting

2 limes
3 grapefruit
6 oranges
Honey, to taste

Juice the limes, grapefruit, and oranges in a citrus press. Stir in
the honey. Makes 4 large glasses.

pine lime and strawberry burst

Serve this divine juice with a frangipani flower peeking coyly over the edge.

orange tropical blossom

4 oranges
1 mango, chopped
1/2 small papaya, peeled, seeded, and chopped
1 1/2 teaspoons orange flower water
Ice cubes, to serve

Juice the oranges in a citrus press. Blend the orange juice, mango, papaya, and orange flower water in a blender until smooth. Serve over ice. Makes 2 medium glasses.

Playing the field can be fun, but so can sitting on the sidelines—especially with a glass of this in your hand.

green and gold

1¹/₃ cups green seedless grapes
6 oranges, peeled
2 lemons, peeled
1 teaspoon honey

Juice the grapes, oranges, and lemons in a juicer. Stir in the honey. Makes 2 large glasses.

An extravaganza of succulent pitted fruit, tempered with the refreshing tang of oranges.

summer orange

3 oranges, peeled
5 small plums, pits removed
4 peaches, pits removed
10 apricots, pits removed

Juice the oranges, plums, peaches, and apricots in a juicer. Stir to combine. Makes 2 large glasses.

If only all of our crushes could be so sweet.

orange citrus crush

12 navel oranges
Zest and juice of 1 lime
Sugar, to taste
Ice cubes, to serve

Segment 2 of the oranges and juice the remainder in a citrus press—don't strain the juice, you can keep the pulp in it. Add the lime zest and juice to the orange juice. Add the orange segments and sugar. Stir to combine and serve over ice. Makes 4 medium glasses.

Note: The juice of navel oranges turns bitter within minutes of juicing, so drink this juice immediately. Use blood oranges when in season.

orange citrus crush

Too old for an ice-cream soda? Go for this grown-up version.

orange sorbet soda

2 cups orange juice
1 cup lemonade

2 to 4 scoops lemon sorbet

Combine the orange juice and lemonade in a pitcher. Pour into 2 large glasses and top each with 1–2 scoops sorbet. Makes 2 large glasses.

All the colors of the fruity rainbow swirled together.

orange and mixed fruit frappé

10 dried apricot halves
1²/₃ cups raspberries
1 banana, chopped
1 mango, chopped
2 cups orange juice
1 tablespoon mint leaves
6 ice cubes

Put the dried apricots in a heatproof bowl with ¹/₄ cup boiling water. Set aside for 10 minutes, or until plump, then drain and roughly chop. Blend the apricots, raspberries, banana, mango, orange juice, mint leaves, and ice cubes in a blender until smooth. Makes 4 medium glasses.

Transport yourself to Sicily, the home of the best blood oranges, with this deeply flavorful juice.

blood orange fruit burst

10 apricots, pits removed
1 1/2 cups strawberries, hulled
1 1/3 cups peeled and seeded lychees
1 1/2 cups blood orange juice
Ice cubes, to serve

Juice the apricots, strawberries, and lychees in a juicer. Stir in the blood orange juice and serve over ice. Makes 2 large glasses.

Vamp it up with ruby-red blood oranges.

blood orange, fennel, and cranberry juice

1 baby fennel
1¹/₂ cups blood orange juice
1¹/₂ cups cranberry juice
Ice cubes, to serve

Juice the baby fennel in a juicer. Stir in the blood orange juice and cranberry juice and serve over ice. Makes 2 large glasses.

orange sorbet soda

Suck it in and prepare for the sour cherry punch.

sweet-tart

1 cup blood orange juice
1/2 cup sour cherry juice
1 tablespoon lime juice
1 cup club soda
Ice cubes, to serve

Combine the blood orange juice, sour cherry juice, and lime juice in a pitcher. Stir in the club soda and serve over ice. Makes 2 large glasses.

The name says it all.

oh, my darlin'

3 clementines or small mandarins
2-inch piece ginger, very thinly sliced
2 cinnamon sticks
Small pinch ground cloves
1½ tablespoons brown sugar

Slice the clementines into rounds and put in a large pitcher. Add the ginger, cinnamon, cloves, brown sugar, and 4 cups boiling water. Stir to combine, pressing against the clementines to help release the juice and flavor. Set aside to infuse for about 10 minutes before serving warm. Makes 4 medium glasses.

You won't know what hit you.

mandarin and passion fruit shots

6 mandarins, peeled
1 large passion fruit

Juice the mandarins in a juicer. Strain the passion fruit pulp and discard the seeds, reserving a few for garnish, if desired. Stir the passion fruit juice into the mandarin juice and chill well. Stir to combine and serve garnished with the reserved passion fruit seeds, if desired. Makes 4 shot glasses.

Just the thing after a tiring afternoon in the park.

mandarin rose

1½ cups mandarin juice
1 teaspoon rose water
2 teaspoons pomegranate syrup
1 cup club soda or lemonade
Ice cubes, to serve

Combine the mandarin juice, rose water, pomegranate syrup, and club soda or lemonade in a pitcher. Serve over ice. Makes 2 large glasses.

mandarin and passion fruit shots

the vegetable garden Just like getting sand between the toes, this chapter is all about getting soil between the teeth. No matter how much you scrub some of these fellas, you'll never convince them to shed

their earthy goodness. After all, you can take the carrot out of the garden but you can't take the garden out of the carrot. The uninitiated may like to start with small servings of these healthy elixirs.

Super-rich in iron and beta-carotene, **beets** are not for the mild-mannered juicer. Cut their earthy richness with citrus. To prepare, give beets a seriously good scrubbing and cut off any green stems. Cut the crown away, chop, and add to the juicer. Sweet **carrots** make a great base juice and are limited only by the fact that they oxidize quickly. Use with citrus juice to help prevent this. Trim tops, then juice. Salty, watery **celery** needs rinsing under running water before juicing; add the leaves, too, if you want. Buy celery with crisp, fresh stems. For sheer refreshing good value, try **cucumber**. Choose firm ones (the variety doesn't matter) with no signs of bruising and store in the refrigerator, wrapped in plastic. No need to peel, just wash and juice. **Fennel** is a funny one. Just when you think you've discovered every way to prepare it, along comes another, such as juicing. Use baby bulbs where possible; larger, more mature ones have a headier flavor. **Garlic** embodies the great and good from the garden. Peel the cloves before you juice. **Green leafy vegetables** like spinach and watercress are excellent sources of antioxidants and phytochemicals. Use leaves straight from the refrigerator while they are still a bit stiff, or juice with other ingredients. Rinse spinach well or soak in ice-cold water for 1 to 2 minutes to get rid of sand and grit. Leaves and **herbs** need to be bundled together or alternated with other, juicier ingredients. Juice on slow. Use good-quality **tomatoes** to get the best flavor and nutritional value.

Add body and bounce to your natural vitality with this spicy little number.

vitalizing beet, carrot, and ginger juice

1 beet, scrubbed
6 carrots
1½-inch piece ginger, peeled

Juice the beet, carrots, and ginger in a juicer. Stir to combine. Makes 2 small glasses.

Down a tumbler of this nourishing blend for a detox that matches style with substance.

dinner in a glass

1 beet, scrubbed
10 to 12 carrots
2 green apples, stalks removed
2 spinach leaves
2 celery stalks

Juice the beet, carrots, apples, spinach, and celery in a juicer. Stir to combine and serve chilled. Makes 2 large glasses.

There's no better way to beet it!

beet, cantaloupe, ginger, and mint juice

6 beets, scrubbed
1/4 medium-size cantaloupe (or other orange-fleshed melon),
    peeled, seeded, and chopped
2 tablespoons roughly chopped ginger
2 tablespoons mint leaves

Juice the beets, cantaloupe, ginger, and mint in a juicer. Stir to combine.
Makes 4 medium glasses.

Too good for you? There's simply no such thing.

too good for you

6 carrots
1 large apple, cored
4 celery stalks, including leaves
6 iceberg lettuce leaves
20 spinach leaves
Ice cubes, to serve

Juice the carrots, apple, celery, lettuce, and spinach in a juicer. Stir to combine and serve over ice. Makes 4 small glasses.

vitalizing beet, carrot, and ginger juice

I can see clearly now that my juicer's here.

honeyed carrots

8 medium carrots
2 cups alfalfa sprouts
4 pears, stalks removed
1 to 2 teaspoons honey, to taste
Carrot strips, for garnish, if desired

Juice the carrots, alfalfa, and pears in a juicer. Stir in the honey. Garnish with carrot strips, if desired. Makes 2 medium glasses.

This orange explosion will get you going in the morning.

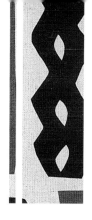

carrot, apricot, and nectarine

8 medium carrots
10 apricots, pits removed
4 large nectarines, pits removed
Ice cubes, to serve
Lemon slices, to serve

Juice the carrots, apricots, and nectarines in a juicer. Stir to combine and serve over ice with lemon slices. Makes 2 large glasses.

When the body isn't the temple it should be, give it a boost with iron-rich tomatoes.

carrot, tomato, lemon, and basil juice

8 medium carrots
4 vine-ripened tomatoes
1 lemon, peeled
1/3 cup basil leaves

Juice the carrots, tomatoes, lemon, and basil in a juicer. Stir to combine.
Makes 2 medium glasses.

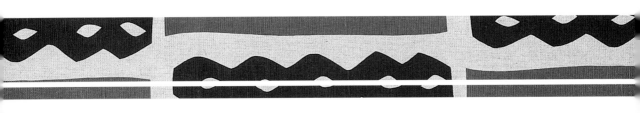

After one cocktail too many, the road to recovery is definitely paved orange.

carrot cocktail 223

10 to 12 medium carrots
1/2 cup pineapple juice
1/2 cup orange juice
1 to 2 teaspoons honey, or to taste
8 ice cubes

Juice the carrots in a juicer. Stir in the pineapple juice, orange juice, honey, and ice cubes. Makes 2 medium glasses.

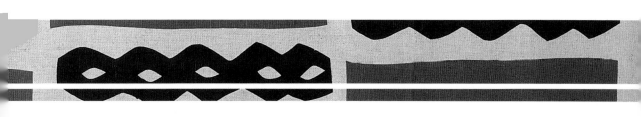

honeyed carrots

Cleanse your palate and freshen your breath with a serious hit of parsley.

celery, parsley, and tomato juice

1 cup parsley
6 vine-ripened tomatoes
4 celery stalks
Celery stalks, extra, to garnish

Juice the parsley, tomatoes, and celery in a juicer. Chill well, then stir to combine. Serve garnished with a celery stalk swizzle stick. Makes 2 large glasses.

Note: For extra spice, add a few drops of hot-pepper sauce and freshly ground black pepper.

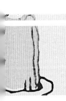
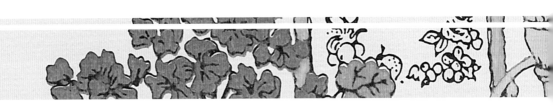

Be a killer queen with this potent concoction and shoot down those germs in style.

cold killer

4 celery stalks
8 medium carrots
2 garlic cloves
1/2 cup Italian parsley
2 teaspoons honey

Juice the celery, carrots, garlic, and parsley in a juicer. Stir in the honey.
Makes 2 medium glasses.

Even the meanest machine needs the occasional tune-up.

green machine

6 celery stalks
2 apples, stalks removed
2 cups alfalfa sprouts
1/2 cup Italian parsley
1/2 cup mint leaves

Juice the celery, apples, alfalfa, parsley, and mint in a juicer. Stir to combine. Makes 2 medium glasses.

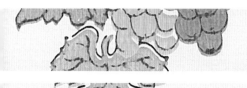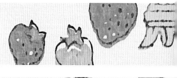

Sticks and stones may break my bones, but juice helps me forget all about it.

sticks and stones

6 celery stalks
5 small peaches, pits removed
1/2 lemon, peeled
1/4 cup basil leaves
Ice cubes, to serve

Juice the celery, peaches, lemon, and basil in a juicer. Stir to combine and serve over ice. Makes 2 medium glasses.

green machine

Don't be a dill, revive and survive with this smart concoction.

cucumber, apple, and dill juice

2 large cucumbers
9 apples, stalks removed
2 tablespoons dill
1 lemon, peeled
Ice cubes, to serve

Juice the cucumbers, apples, dill, and lemon in a juicer. Stir to combine
and serve over ice. Makes 2 medium glasses.

Enhance your cool factor with a chilled shot of cucumber.

cool as a cucumber

3 large cucumbers
3 limes, peeled
1 cup mint leaves
1 1/2 tablespoons superfine sugar

Juice the cucumbers, limes, and mint in a juicer. Stir in the sugar. Makes 2 large glasses.

Beet yourself up at the end of winter and get yourself into the mood for spring.

spring clean

2 large cucumbers, peeled
6 carrots
1 large green apple, stalk removed
2 celery stalks, including leaves
1 large beet, scrubbed
Ice cubes, to serve

Juice the cucumbers, carrots, apple, celery, and beet in a juicer. Stir to combine and serve over ice. Makes 4 small glasses.

Calm the troubled waters of your tummy with this gentle, soothing tonic.

savory soother

7 medium cucumbers
1 lime, peeled
1/3 cup cilantro leaves
1 garlic clove
1 small avocado, peeled, pit removed
Large pinch ground cumin

Juice the cucumbers, lime, coriander, and garlic in a juicer. Transfer to a blender, add the avocado and cumin, and blend until smooth. Makes 2 small glasses.

cool as a cucumber

Tender young fennel bulbs add a fresh, astringent licorice kick to good old apple and orange juice.

fennel, apple, and orange juice

1 baby fennel, outer leaves removed
3 apples, stalks removed
6 oranges, peeled
¼ cup basil leaves
1 teaspoon honey, optional

Juice the fennel, apples, oranges, and basil in a juicer. Stir in the honey, if desired. Makes 2 large glasses.

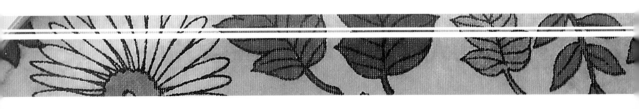

For a licorice sting, choose a larger bulb of fennel.

fennel and orange juice

8 oranges
1 baby fennel, outer leaves removed

Peel and quarter the oranges. Juice the fennel in a juicer to release the flavors, then juice the oranges and chill well. Stir to combine. Makes 2 medium glasses.

Note: When in season, larger, more developed fennel will have a stronger flavor than baby fennel.

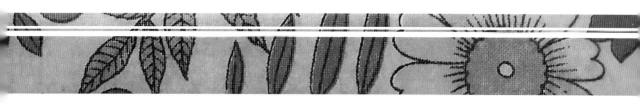

Your mom always told you to eat your greens, but better still, drink them!

green shot

1 1/2 cups Italian parsley
1 medium cucumber
1/2 teaspoon superfine sugar
1/2 teaspoon lemon juice

Juice the parsley and cucumber in a juicer, saving a little cucumber for garnishing. Add the sugar and stir until fully dissolved. Chill well, then stir in the lemon juice and garnish with cucumber sticks. Serve immediately. Makes 6 shot glasses.

One, two, three . . . down the hatch.

herbal tonic

1 cup Italian parsley
1 cup mint leaves
1/2 cup cilantro leaves
1 1/4-inch piece ginger
2 cups tonic water
Ice cubes, to serve

Juice the parsley, mint, cilantro, and ginger in a juicer, then add 2
tablespoons water to help push the juice through. Stir in the tonic water
and serve over ice. Makes 2 large glasses.

green shot

Why didn't we know of this blend when we were younger? Prepare and drink just before heading out.

basil, spearmint, and licorice wake-me-up

1 tablespoon licorice tea leaves
1 tablespoon spearmint tea leaves
10 basil leaves, plus extra for garnish

Put the licorice and spearmint tea leaves into a teapot. Lightly crush the basil leaves and add them to the pot. Fill the pot with boiling water (about 4 cups), cover, and leave to brew for 3 minutes. Strain into teacups and garnish with basil leaves. Serve hot or cold. Makes 2 glasses.

Note: As the tea cools, the licorice flavor becomes stronger and sweeter—add a few slices of lemon if you find it too strong.

Mint juleps are just the ticket when the in-laws visit, but try to stay off the bourbon.

mint julep

1 cup mint leaves, roughly chopped,
    plus whole leaves for garnish
1 tablespoon sugar
1 tablespoon lemon juice
1 cup pineapple juice
1 cup ginger ale
Ice cubes, to serve

Roughly chop the mint leaves and place in a heatproof pitcher with the sugar. Using a wooden spoon, bruise the mint. Add the lemon juice, pineapple juice, and 1/2 cup boiling water and mix well. Cover with plastic wrap and set aside for 30 minutes. Strain, then chill. Just before serving, stir in the ginger ale. Serve over ice, garnished with mint leaves. Makes 2 medium glasses.

Sweet memories in a glass.

rosemary and apple infusion

12 apples, juiced and strained, or 4 cups bottled apple juice
1 sprig rosemary
¼ cup superfine sugar

Combine the apple juice, rosemary, and sugar in a large saucepan over high heat and stir until the sugar has dissolved. Bring to a boil, then remove from the heat. Allow to infuse for at least 1 minute, depending on your preferred strength of rosemary flavor. Strain and serve either warm or well chilled. Makes 4 medium glasses.

Are you going to Scarborough Fair?

sage, rosemary, celery, and carrot juice

2½ tablespoons sage leaves
2½ tablespoons rosemary leaves
8 celery stalks
3 carrots
Ice cubes, to serve

Juice the sage, rosemary, celery, and carrots in a juicer in that order so that the vegetables help to push the herb juice through. Stir to combine and serve over ice. Makes 2 medium glasses.

basil, spearmint, and licorice wake-me-up

Life can be a marathon *and* a sprint, so when you need a fuel injection, reach for the juicer.

spinach energizer

2 cups baby spinach leaves
1 large cucumber
3 apples, stalks removed
3 celery stalks
1 baby fennel
1/2 cup parsley

Juice the spinach, cucumber, apples, celery, fennel, and parsley in a juicer.
Stir to combine. Makes 2 large glasses.

Butterflies can flutter at any time. Soothe them away with this calming tonic.

tummy calmer

2 cups spinach leaves
¼ small cabbage
4 apples, stalks removed

Juice the spinach, cabbage, and apples in a juicer. Stir to combine. Makes 2 small glasses.

Prepare for blastoff.

rocket fuel

3 cups arugula leaves
1/2 cup mint leaves
1/2-inch piece ginger
1/2 garlic clove
pinch ground cumin
1 1/4 cups apple juice

Juice the arugula, mint, ginger, and garlic in a juicer, then add 1 tablespoon water to help push the juice through. Stir in the cumin and apple juice. Makes 4 shot glasses.

How's this for a good intestinal cleanser?

waterworks

1 cup watercress leaves
4 celery stalks
1 scallion, chopped
1¹/₂ cucumbers
Ice cubes, to serve

Juice the watercress, celery, scallion, and cucumber in a juicer. Stir to combine and serve over ice. Makes 2 medium glasses.

spinach energizer

Spicy, hot, and red in tooth and claw.

gazpacho in a glass

6 vine-ripened tomatoes
1 red pepper
1 lemon, peeled
2 large cucumbers
1/2 cup parsley
1 garlic clove
Dash hot-pepper sauce
Ice cubes, to serve
Extra-virgin olive oil, to serve, optional

Juice the tomatoes, red pepper, lemon, cucumbers, parsley, and garlic in
a juicer. Stir in the hot-pepper sauce to taste. Serve over ice with a drizzle
of extra-virgin olive oil, if desired. Makes 2 large glasses.

This drink is a seriously good tipple in its own right, but if you must add a slug of vodka, we promise not to tell.

virgin mary

3 cups tomato juice
1 tablespoon Worcestershire sauce
2 tablespoons lemon juice
1/4 teaspoon ground nutmeg
Few drops hot-pepper sauce
12 ice cubes
2 lemon slices, halved
Salt and pepper, to taste

Put the tomato juice, Worcestershire sauce, lemon juice, nutmeg, and hot-pepper sauce in a large pitcher and stir to combine. Blend the ice cubes in a blender for 30 seconds, or until the ice is crushed to 1/2 cup. Pour the tomato juice mixture into 4 glasses and add the crushed ice and lemon slices. Season with salt and pepper. Makes 4 small glasses.

For those days when you just can't make up your mind.

sweet and sour

4 vine-ripened tomatoes
3 oranges, peeled
1/2 cup mint leaves
1 teaspoon superfine sugar
1 teaspoon balsamic vinegar
Ice cubes, to serve

Juice the tomatoes, oranges, and mint leaves in a juicer. Stir in the sugar and balsamic vinegar until the sugar has dissolved. Serve over ice. Makes 2 medium glasses.

This is no ordinary tomato juice. It's much bigger than that.

big red

1 cup tomato juice
1 cup apricot nectar
Large pinch ground ginger
Pinch ground cardamom
Small pinch ground cloves
Ice cubes, to serve

Combine the tomato juice, apricot nectar, ginger, cardamom, and cloves in a large pitcher; chill well. Stir to combine and serve over ice. Makes 2 large glasses.

gazpacho in a glass

cinnamon, spice, and all things nice The spice cupboard is a many splendored thing: cloves and vanilla beans, cardamom pods, cinnamon sticks, and aromatic nutmeg. Pound or grind, pulp and

chop, blend and infuse your way to soothing brews. But not every juice has to be all snap and crackle. Look deep into your cupboard and discover ingredients full of depth and character, just waiting their turn.

Luxuriously aromatic, flower waters such as orange and rose are only needed in small amounts. Follow recipe suggestions. Fresh flowers such as lavender and edible rose petals are also useful: infuse and strain. Good old ginger. Knobbly, beige-colored, and a rhizome to boot, but still we can't get enough of it. With good reason, too: it calms an upset tummy, aids the digestion, and gets a sluggish circulation into action. Generally, no need to peel or slice, just wash and use in the juicer. If it's fibrous, it may be easier to grate. Ground spices such as cardamom, cinnamon, cloves, and cumin are great for adding warmth and depth to drinks. In their whole form, cardamom pods and cinnamon sticks can be used in infused drinks; freshly grated nutmeg brings a spicy warmth; and star anise adds a mild licorice edge to drinks. For the best flavor, use the fresh spice if possible and grind it yourself as needed. A sticky, sweet-sour pulp, tamarind is sold in blocks that contain the plant's seeds or as ready-made concentrated paste in jars. To use, cut off a little, mix with hot water, then press through a sieve with a spoon to extract the pulp. Store in the refrigerator for up to a year. The humble tea bag isn't so humble after all. In infusions they go particularly well with citrus and fresh herbs. Good-quality vanilla pods have a warm, caramel vanilla aroma and flavor, and should be soft, not hard or dry. You can also use natural vanilla extract, but beware of cheap copies. The pod can be reused: wash in cold water, then dry and store.

Use honey and vanilla to coax out the natural sweetness of the humble carrot.

cardamom, carrot, and orange juice

8 medium carrots
6 oranges, peeled
Small pinch ground cardamom
1 teaspoon natural vanilla extract
1 teaspoon honey
Ice cubes, to serve

Juice the carrots and oranges in a juicer. Stir in the cardamom, vanilla, and honey. Serve over ice. Makes 2 large glasses.

Subtly spiced, this refreshing tea is a perfect match for a light lunch and salad.

cardamom and orange tea

3 cardamom pods
1 cup orange juice
3 strips orange zest
2 tablespoons superfine sugar
Ice cubes, to serve

Put the cardamom pods on a chopping board and crack them open by pressing with the side of a large knife. Put the cardamom, orange juice, orange zest, sugar, and 2 cups water into a pan. Stir over medium heat for 10 minutes, or until the sugar has dissolved. Bring to a boil, then remove from the heat. Set aside to infuse for 2–3 hours, or until cool, then refrigerate. Strain and serve over ice. Makes 2 medium glasses.

Use the best-quality maple syrup you can find, then make this for your favorite Mountie.

cinnamon, maple, and pear frappé

6 canned pear halves in natural juice (about 1 1/2 cups)
1/2 teaspoon ground cinnamon
1 1/2 tablespoons pure maple syrup
12 large ice cubes

Blend the pears and juice, cinnamon, maple syrup, and ice cubes in a blender until smooth. Makes 2 large glasses.

Steeping the fruit and spices deepens the flavor of this golden infusion.

cinnamon and apple tea infusion

1 cinnamon stick
4 Golden Delicious apples, roughly chopped
3 to 4 tablespoons brown sugar
Ice cubes, to serve

Put the cinnamon stick, apples, brown sugar, and 4 cups water into a pan. Bring to a boil, then reduce the heat and gently simmer for 10–15 minutes, or until the flavors have infused and the apple has softened. Remove from the heat and cool slightly, then chill. Strain and serve over lots of ice. Makes 2 medium glasses.

cinnamon, maple, and pear frappé

Carrot and lime receive a fragrant lift with the addition of rose water and cinnamon in this *Arabian Nights*–inspired drink.

rose water, carrot, and lime juice

12 medium carrots
3 limes, peeled
1 teaspoon rose water
Large pinch ground cinnamon
Ice cubes, to serve

Juice the carrots and limes in a juicer. Stir in the rose water and cinnamon and serve over ice. Makes 2 medium glasses.

Sweet and exotic, this juice is perfect for a languid late-afternoon tea.

turkish delight

2 to 3 lemons, or to taste
1 teaspoon rose water
2 teaspoons honey
Ice cubes, to serve

Juice the lemons in a citrus press. Stir in the rose water, honey, and 1 1/2 cups cold water. Serve over ice. Makes 2 large glasses.

Play it again, Sam. Evoke the romance of *Casablanca* with this fragrant and exotic juice.

orange blossom citrus refresher

6 oranges, peeled
1 cup mint leaves
1 1/2 teaspoons orange flower water
1 teaspoon pomegranate syrup, plus extra to serve,
    optional
Ice cubes, to serve
Mint sprigs, to garnish

Juice the oranges and mint leaves in a juicer. Stir in the orange flower water and the 1 teaspoon pomegranate syrup. Serve over ice, garnished with mint. Drizzle with a little more pomegranate syrup, if desired. Makes 2 medium glasses.

Create your own costume drama with this ladylike tonic.

lavender and rose lemonade

Juice and zest of 2 lemons
25 English lavender flowers, stripped from their stems
1 1/2 cups sugar
1/2 teaspoon rose water
Edible pale pink rose petals, to garnish, optional

Put the lemon zest, lavender flowers, sugar, and 2 cups boiling water into a heatproof pitcher and mix well. Cover with plastic wrap and set aside for 15 minutes. Strain, then stir in the lemon juice, rose water, and enough cold water to make 4 cups. Chill well. Stir to combine and serve garnished with rose petals, if desired. Makes 6 small glasses.

Note: For a milder flavor, add more water.

lavender and rose lemonade

Strong and spicy, line up the shot glasses and find out who's the real tough guy.

red ginger

2³/₄ cups red seedless grapes
10 small plums, pits removed
2 limes, peeled
1¹/₄-inch piece ginger
¹/₂ cup mint leaves
Ice cubes, to serve

Juice the grapes, plums, limes, ginger, and mint in a juicer. Stir to combine and serve over ice. Makes 4 shot glasses.

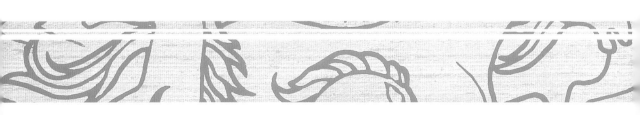

Just what you need to get yourself into gear when time is short and the to-do list is long.

pineapple ginger kick

1/2 pineapple, peeled
3 oranges, peeled
1 1/2-inch piece ginger
Ice cubes, to serve

Juice the pineapple, oranges, and ginger in a juicer. Stir to combine and serve over ice. Makes 2 small glasses.

279

Recover in style with the ultimate tummy soother.

ginger, lemon, and mint soother

3/4-inch piece ginger, thinly sliced
1/2 cup lemon juice
2 1/2 tablespoons honey
1 tablespoon mint leaves
Ice cubes, to serve

Put the ginger, lemon juice, honey, mint, and 3 cups boiling water into a heatproof pitcher. Set aside to infuse for 2–3 hours, or until cool. Strain and chill. Stir to combine and serve over ice. Makes 4 small glasses.

Note: This drink is delicious served the next day, as all the flavors will have had time to infuse.

In need of a little get-up-and-go? Try a little of this.

gingered melon juice

1 honeydew melon, peeled, seeded, and chopped
1 cantaloupe (or other orange-fleshed melon), peeled,
    seeded, and chopped
3/4-inch piece ginger

Juice the honeydew, cantaloupe, and ginger in a juicer. Stir to combine.
Makes 2 large glasses.

red ginger

Instant winter warming with a zing of ginger and a healthy
dose of vitamins.

warm ginger and carrot shots

16 medium carrots
1½-inch piece ginger
1 tablespoon lemon juice
Large pinch ground cinnamon
Large pinch ground cumin
Plain yogurt, to serve, optional

Juice the carrots and ginger in a juicer. Transfer to a saucepan with the
lemon juice, cinnamon, and cumin. Stir over medium heat until just
warmed through, then pour into shot glasses or tall glasses. Top each
glass with a small dollop of yogurt and slightly swirl through. Makes 8
shot glasses or 2 large glasses.

Breathe deep and inhale the soothing aromas—a dreamy break is on its way.

ginger and lemon calm

1¼-inch piece ginger, sliced
1 lemon, thinly sliced
1 chamomile tea bag
Honey, to taste

Put the ginger, lemon, and tea bag in the bottom of a heatproof bowl and pour in 4 cups boiling water. Set aside to infuse for 10 minutes before straining. Serve with a little honey. Makes 4 small glasses.

Flush away any irritations with this spicy, cleansing tonic.

spiced cranberry infusion

4 cups cranberry juice
1/3 cup superfine sugar
2-inch piece ginger, sliced
3 strips orange zest
2 cinnamon sticks
Small pinch ground cloves
Orange slices, to garnish, optional

Put the cranberry juice, sugar, ginger, orange zest, cinnamon sticks, and cloves into a large saucepan. Stir over high heat until the sugar has dissolved. Bring to a boil, then turn off the heat but leave on the stovetop to infuse for 15 minutes. Strain and serve warm, garnished with a slice of orange, if desired. Makes 4 small glasses.

This is just the ticket to help you through an afternoon slump.

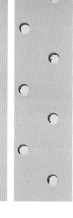

warm ginger zinger

4-inch piece ginger, very thinly sliced
1 teaspoon white peppercorns
1 star anise
1 cinnamon stick
Honey, to taste

Put the ginger, peppercorns, star anise, and cinnamon in a large heatproof pitcher and pour in 4 cups boiling water. Set aside to infuse for about 15 minutes. Serve with honey. Makes 4 medium glasses.

warm ginger and carrot shots

You know it's good for you, but you never knew it could taste so darn good.

iced kiwifruit green tea

6 kiwifruit, peeled, plus extra slices to serve
1 lemon, thinly sliced, plus extra slices to serve
2 green tea bags
2 tablespoons superfine sugar
Ice cubes, to serve

Juice the 6 kiwifruit in a juicer. Put the lemon slices, tea bags, and 5 cups boiling water into a heatproof bowl. Set aside to infuse for 5 minutes. Strain and discard the tea bags. Add the kiwifruit juice and sugar and stir until the sugar has dissolved. Set aside to cool, then chill. Stir to combine and serve over ice, garnished with a slice each of kiwifruit and lemon. Makes 4 medium glasses.

If no one is watching, pop the tea bags over your eyes while you wait for this refreshing brew to chill.

iced lemon and peppermint tea

2 peppermint tea bags
6 thick strips lemon zest
1 tablespoon sugar, or to taste
Ice cubes, to serve
Mint leaves, to garnish

Put the tea bags, lemon zest, and 3 1/3 cups boiling water into a heatproof bowl. Set aside to infuse for 5 minutes. Squeeze out and discard the tea bags. Stir in the sugar and chill. Stir to combine and serve over ice, garnished with mint leaves. Makes 2 medium glasses.

Note: Alternatively, pour about 1/2 cup of the tea mixture into the holes of an ice-cube tray. Freeze and serve with the chilled tea.

This herbal hit will have you skipping all the way to work.

iced mint tea

4 peppermint tea bags
1/3 cup honey
2 cups grapefruit juice
1 cup orange juice
Mint sprigs, to garnish

Put the tea bags and 3 cups boiling water into a large heatproof pitcher. Set aside to infuse for 3 minutes. Discard the tea bags. Stir in the honey and set aside to cool. Add the grapefruit and orange juices, cover, and chill. Stir to combine and serve garnished with mint sprigs. Makes 6 small glasses.

Develop a taste for island living with this piquant brew.

minty pineapple iced tea

1 pineapple, or 2 cups pineapple juice
2 English breakfast tea bags
$1/2$ cup mint leaves
Ice cubes, to serve
Mint sprigs, to garnish

Juice the pineapple in a juicer, then strain the juice. Put the tea bags, mint leaves, and 5 cups boiling water into a large heatproof bowl. Set aside to infuse for 5 minutes. Discard the tea bags and mint. Stir in the pineapple juice and chill. Stir to combine and serve over ice, garnished with mint sprigs. Makes 4 medium glasses.

iced kiwifruit green tea

Sweet yet subtle, this is a brew to daydream over.

iced orange and strawberry tea

3 oranges, peeled
2³/4 cups strawberries, hulled
2 orange pekoe tea bags
Ice cubes, to serve
Orange zest, to garnish, optional

Juice the oranges and strawberries in a juicer. Put the tea bags and 5 cups boiling water in a heatproof bowl. Set aside to infuse for 5 minutes. Discard the tea bags. Stir in the orange and strawberry juice. Chill well. Stir to combine and serve over ice with a twist of orange zest, if desired. Makes 4 medium glasses.

Darjeeling, darling, is the only tea in town.

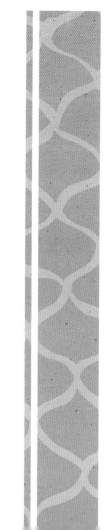

orange and ginger tea cooler

1 tablespoon Darjeeling tea leaves
Zest of 1 small orange, cut into long, thin strips
1 cup ginger ale
8 thin slices glacé ginger
2 tablespoons sugar
4 to 6 ice cubes
Mint leaves, to garnish

Put the tea leaves, half the orange zest, and 2 cups boiling water in a heatproof bowl. Cover and set aside to infuse for 5 minutes. Strain through a fine strainer into a pitcher. Add the ginger ale, stir, and chill for 6 hours—preferably overnight. An hour before serving, stir in the glacé ginger, sugar, and remaining orange zest. Stir to combine, pour into tall glasses, add 2 or 3 ice cubes per glass, and garnish with mint leaves. Makes 2 medium glasses.

When you fancy an old-fashioned afternoon tea party, sip this on the porch and see who comes a-knockin'.

american iced tea

4 Ceylon tea bags
2 tablespoons sugar
2 tablespoons lemon juice
1 1/2 cups dark grape juice
2 cups orange juice
1 1/2 cups ginger ale
Ice cubes, to serve
Lemon slices, to serve

Put the tea bags and 4 cups boiling water in a heatproof bowl. Set aside to infuse for 3 minutes. Discard the tea bags. Add the sugar and set aside to cool. Stir in the lemon, grape, and orange juices, then chill. Stir in the ginger ale and serve over ice with a slice of lemon. Makes 8 small glasses.

Smoky and seductive, this sophisticated tea makes storm clouds disappear.

earl grey summer tea

1 cup orange juice
2 teaspoons finely grated orange zest
1 tablespoon Earl Grey tea leaves
1 cinnamon stick, plus 4 to garnish
2 tablespoons sugar, or to taste
Ice cubes, to serve
1 orange, thinly sliced into rounds

Put the orange juice, orange zest, tea leaves, 1 cinnamon stick, and 3 cups water into a medium saucepan. Slowly bring to a simmer over low heat. Add the sugar and stir until dissolved. Remove from the heat and set aside to cool. Strain the liquid into a pitcher and chill. Stir to combine and serve with lots of ice cubes, garnished with the orange slices and extra cinnamon sticks. Makes 4 small glasses.

iced orange and strawberry tea

Classy as a cordial, this syrup also makes a divine sorbet.

lime and lemon grass syrup

4 limes
3 to 4 stems lemon grass, bruised and cut into 4-inch lengths
2-inch piece ginger, chopped
2/3 cup superfine sugar

Juice the limes in a citrus press. Put the lime juice, lemon grass, ginger, sugar, and 8 cups water in a large saucepan. Stir over high heat until the sugar has dissolved. Bring to a boil and cook for 1 1/2 hours, or until reduced to about 1 1/2 cups. Set aside to cool, then strain. Makes 1 1/2 cups.

Note: To serve, pour a little syrup into a glass with ice and top with club soda or lemonade. Use stems of lemon grass as swizzle sticks.

A fragrant tonic for the soul as well as the body.

citrus and lemon grass tea

3 stems lemon grass
2 slices lemon, plus extra to serve
3 teaspoons honey, or to taste
Ice cubes, to serve

Discard the first two tough outer layers of the lemon grass. Thinly slice the lemon grass and put into a heatproof pitcher with 2 1/2 cups boiling water. Add 2 lemon slices, cover, and set aside to infuse and cool to room temperature. Strain, stir in the honey, and chill. Stir to combine and serve over ice with lemon slices. Makes 2 medium glasses.

Note: For maximum flavor, only use the bottom third of the lemon grass stems (the white part). Use the trimmed stems as a garnish.

Mouth-puckeringly tart when straight, a dash of sugar makes tamarind lip-smackingly good.

tamarind cooler

2 teaspoons tamarind concentrate
3 tablespoons superfine sugar
1 cup mint leaves
12 large ice cubes

Blend the tamarind, sugar, mint, ice cubes, and 1 cup water in a blender until smooth. Makes 2 medium glasses.

A great winter blend, this will soon have you feeling warm and calm all over.

vanilla and apricot orange infusion

1¼ cups chopped dried apricots
1 vanilla bean, chopped
Zest of 1 orange
¼ cup superfine sugar
Small pinch cloves, optional
Ice cubes, to serve

Combine the apricots, vanilla bean, orange zest, sugar, cloves, and 12 cups water in a large saucepan. Stir over high heat until the sugar has dissolved. Bring to a boil, reduce the heat, and gently simmer for 20 minutes. Set aside to cool. Strain and chill well. Stir to combine and serve over ice. Makes 6 medium glasses.

vanilla and apricot orange infusion

creamy concoctions Welcome to the world of the blender. A place of creamy, dreamy, silky, smoothy, cruisy, woozy, bluesy blends. We're talking no more Mr. Second Fiddle, no more Mr. Waiting in the Wings

for the blender—dairy-based drinks are where it's at. Low-fat, no-fat, whole-cream milk, even buttermilk: it loves them all. Fruit yogurts, frozen yogurts: perfect! Ice cream: delicious!

Weighing in at around 10 percent fat content, ice cream adds

an unbeatable rich and creamy texture to smoothies. The better quality

the ice cream, the better the resulting drink. Homemade ice creams

made with raw eggs should be eaten within three days. Those without

eggs will keep for longer, but their flavor may change as they age. Be it

skim, low-fat, or whole, milk is the bedrock upon which all other

smoothies stand. Packed with calcium, protein, and vitamins A and D, it

combines well with everything from macadamia nuts to figs. Lower-fat

milks result in a more watery drink. Buttermilk is made from pasteurized

skim milk, to which an acid-producing bacteria is added, thickening it

and giving it a tangy taste. If using buttermilk in place of whole milk,

omit any lemon or lime. Live yogurt can support the digestive

system by restoring natural gut bacteria. Of course, it also tastes good.

Blend with well-established winners such as bananas, mangoes, and

limes, but also try dried apricots, avocados, and prunes. Don't worry if

the low-fat wildberry yogurt required by a recipe isn't available. Choose

a similar one; the result will be just as good. Smoothies are ideal places

for healthy additives to hide. Try sweet-tasting malted milk

powder, made from dried and ground barley grains, or raw wheat germ,

the extracted embryo of the wheat grain. Store wheat germ in the

refrigerator—otherwise it will go rancid because of its high oil content.

Buy both at health food stores.

Best consumed on a Sunday with the newspaper in one hand and some waffles in the other.

blue maple

1 cup low-fat blueberry fromage frais
3/4 cup low-fat milk
1 tablespoon maple syrup
1/2 teaspoon ground cinnamon
2 cups frozen blueberries

Blend the fromage frais, milk, maple syrup, cinnamon, and all but a few of the frozen blueberries in a blender until smooth. Serve topped with the remaining blueberries. Makes 2 medium glasses.

It's creamy, it's cold, and it's berry, berry good.

berry slushy

2 cups frozen blueberries
1¼ cups raspberries
¾ cup vanilla yogurt
1 cup milk
1 tablespoon wheat germ

Blend the frozen blueberries in a blender in short bursts until starting to break up. Add the raspberries, yogurt, milk, and wheat germ and blend until smooth. Makes 2 large glasses.

Comfort yourself with a little pink milk at bedtime.

long tall raspberry and blueberry

1²/3 cups raspberries
1¹/3 cups blueberries
2 cups milk

Chill 2 or 3 tall glasses in the freezer for 20 minutes. Blend the raspberries and blueberries in a blender until smooth. Pour about ¼ cup of the berry purée into a pitcher and carefully swirl in a spiral pattern around the inside of each glass; return glasses to the freezer. Add the milk to the remaining berry purée in the blender and blend until thick and creamy. Pour into the glasses and serve. Makes 2 large glasses.

Note: Any berry is suitable for this drink. When in season, try mulberries. Depending on the sweetness of the berries, you may want to add a little honey. Even those who are lactose-intolerant can enjoy this drink—it is delicious made with rice milk.

Give 'em the old razzle-dazzle and watch 'em return for more.

razzle-dazzle

1 lime
1¹/4 cups raspberries
1 teaspoon natural vanilla extract
3/4 cup strawberry frozen yogurt

Juice the lime in a citrus press. Blend the raspberries, lime juice, vanilla, and frozen yogurt in a blender until smooth. Makes 2 small glasses.

blue maple

Whip these up for the kids and you'll be the fairy godmother.

apple and black currant shake

1 cup apple and black currant juice
2 tablespoons plain yogurt
3/4 cup milk
3 scoops vanilla ice cream

Blend the juice, yogurt, milk, and ice cream in a blender until well combined and fluffy. Makes 2 medium glasses.

No one can be peachy keen all the time, so fake it in style.

peachy keen

2 large peaches, chopped
1/2 cup raspberries
3/4 cup low-fat peach and mango yogurt
3/4 cup apricot nectar
8 large ice cubes
Peach wedges, to serve

Blend the chopped peaches, raspberries, yogurt, apricot nectar, and ice cubes in a blender until thick and smooth. Serve with the peach wedges. Makes 2 medium glasses.

The ultimate classic combo, this version gives peaches and cream a modern makeover.

peach nectar fluff

2^1/$_2$ cups peach nectar
2^1/$_2$ cups club soda
4 scoops vanilla ice cream
1 peach, sliced

Combine the peach nectar and club soda in a pitcher. Pour into 4 tall glasses, top each with a scoop of ice cream, and garnish with a slice of peach. Makes 4 medium glasses.

Just when winter thinks it's got you cornered, strike back with vitamin-rich, sweet dried fruit.

pear and peach protein drink

3 dried pear halves
3 dried peach halves
1 egg
2 tablespoons low-fat peach yogurt
1 1/2 cups skim milk
1 tablespoon malted milk powder
1 tablespoon ground almonds
Ground cinnamon, to serve

Put the pears, peaches, and 1/2 cup boiling water into a heatproof bowl. Set aside for 10 minutes, or until the fruit is plump and juicy. Drain the fruit, reserving the soaking liquid, and allow to cool. Chop the fruit and blend with the soaking liquid, egg, yogurt, milk, malted milk powder, and almonds in a blender until thick and smooth. Serve sprinkled with a little cinnamon. Makes 2 medium glasses.

apple and black currant shake

Let this mineral-rich smoothie work its magic on any wayward moods or blood-sugar levels.

banana and berry vanilla smoothie

2 bananas, chopped
1 1/3 cups mixed berries

3 tablespoons low-fat vanilla fromage frais or whipped yogurt
2 cups skim milk
1 tablespoon oat bran

Blend the banana, berries, fromage frais, milk, and oat bran in a blender for 2 minutes, or until thick and creamy. Makes 2 medium glasses.

Note: The smoothie will be thicker if you use frozen berries. You may need to add an extra 1/2 cup skim milk to thin it down.

Go low on fat but keep the full-on flavor with this mineral-rich revitalizer.

banana date smoothie

2 bananas, chopped
1/3 cup fresh dates, pitted and chopped
1 cup low-fat plain yogurt
1/2 cup skim milk
8 ice cubes

Blend the bananas, dates, yogurt, milk, and ice cubes in a blender until smooth. Makes 2 medium glasses.

We could all do with one of these!

good start to the day

2 bananas, chopped
1 large mango, chopped
2 cups skim milk
2 cups orange juice or pink grapefruit juice

Blend the bananas, mango, milk, and orange or pink grapefruit juice in a blender until smooth. Pour into a pitcher and chill. Makes 4 small glasses.

The sort of drink to make us go weak at the knees.

caramelized banana shake

2 bananas, chopped
2 cups milk
2 scoops ice cream
1 1/2 tablespoons caramel sauce
1 tablespoon malted milk powder
Pinch ground cinnamon

Blend the bananas, milk, ice cream, caramel sauce, malted milk powder,
and cinnamon in a blender until smooth. Makes 2 large glasses.

good start to the day

Pop the blueberry bubbles for a tongue-tingling explosion.

mango smoothie with fresh berries

2 mangoes, chopped
1/2 cup milk
1 cup buttermilk
1 tablespoon superfine sugar
2 scoops mango gelato or sorbet
1/3 cup blueberries

Blend the mango, milk, buttermilk, sugar, and gelato in a blender until smooth. Serve garnished with the blueberries. Makes 4 small glasses.

Blend away for a fresh and spicy blast.

spiced mango lassi

3 mangoes, chopped
1 cup plain yogurt
1 cup milk
1 teaspoon honey
1 teaspoon ground cinnamon
1/2 teaspoon ground cardamom

Blend the mango, yogurt, milk, honey, cinnamon, and cardamom in a blender until thick and smooth. Makes 2 medium glasses.

Note: Lassis are popular drinks in India, where they are served alongside curries—the yogurt cools and cleanses the palate. They can also be made with buttermilk.

Do the hippy hippy shake with a luscious mound of melon.

melon shake

1/2 small cantaloupe (or other orange-fleshed melon), peeled,
    seeded, and chopped
5 scoops vanilla ice cream
11/2 cups milk
2 tablespoons honey
Ground nutmeg, to serve

Blend the cantaloupe in a blender for 30 seconds, or until smooth. Add
the ice cream, milk, and honey and blend for another 10–20 seconds, or
until well combined and smooth. Serve sprinkled with ground nutmeg.
Makes 2 medium glasses.

Light, juicy watermelon cuts through the creaminess of this indulgent blend. Making it all right, right?

watermelon smoothie

3 cups chopped watermelon
1/2 cup yogurt
1 cup milk
1 tablespoon superfine sugar
2 scoops vanilla ice cream

Blend the watermelon, yogurt, milk, and sugar in a blender until smooth. Add the ice cream and blend for a few seconds, or until frothy. Makes 4 small glasses.

Note: Use seedless watermelon if possible. Otherwise, pick out as many seeds as you can before blending.

watermelon smoothie

Start the day in a relaxed way with this vitamin B–rich cocktail.

passion fruit breakfast shake

1 passion fruit and 2 to 3 pieces other mixed fruit (mangoes,
    bananas, peaches, strawberries, blueberries)

¼ cup vanilla yogurt
1 cup milk
2 teaspoons wheat germ
1 tablespoon honey
1 egg, optional
1 tablespoon malted milk powder

Blend the fruit, yogurt, milk, wheat germ, honey, egg, and malted milk
powder in a blender for 30–60 seconds, or until well combined. Makes
2 medium glasses.

Intense but smooth. It's kinda nice like that.

passion fruit and vanilla ice cream smoothie

2/3 cup canned passion fruit pulp in syrup
1/2 cup coconut milk
1 cup milk
1/4 cup dried coconut
1/4 teaspoon natural vanilla extract
3 scoops vanilla ice cream

Blend half the passion fruit pulp, the coconut milk, milk, coconut, vanilla, and ice cream in a blender until smooth and fluffy. Stir in the remaining passion fruit pulp. Makes 2 medium glasses.

Serve in parfait glasses with long spoons and curly straws for the genuine diner experience.

passion fruit and vanilla ice cream whip

4 passion fruit
$1/3$ cup passion fruit yogurt
2 cups milk
1 tablespoon superfine sugar
2 to 4 scoops vanilla ice cream

Push the passion fruit pulp through a sieve to remove the seeds. Transfer to a blender with the yogurt, milk, sugar, and 2 scoops of ice cream and blend until smooth. Pour into 2 glasses and top each with an extra scoop of ice cream, if desired. Makes 2 medium glasses.

Finish this off with a generous dribble of homemade passion fruit syrup—and let it finish you off.

passion fruit ice cream soda

6 passion fruit
2¹/₂ cups lemonade
2 to 4 scoops vanilla ice cream

Combine the passion fruit pulp (you will need ¹/₂ cup) with the lemonade. Pour into 2 glasses and top each with 1 or 2 scoops of ice cream. Serve with straws and long spoons. Makes 2 large glasses.

passion fruit ice cream soda

Once you get started you may not be able to stop, so make sure there's plenty to go around.

blueberry starter

1^1/$_3$ cups blueberries
1 cup plain yogurt
1 cup milk
1 tablespoon wheat germ
1 to 2 teaspoons honey, to taste

Blend the blueberries, yogurt, milk, wheat germ, and honey in a blender until smooth. Makes 2 medium glasses.

Note: Frozen blueberries are great for this recipe. There is no need to thaw them before use.

A knockout serve, with berries for sweetener.

mixed berry protein punch

2 cups mixed berries (strawberries, raspberries, blueberries)
1 tablespoon protein powder
3/4 cup vanilla yogurt
1 1/2 cups milk
2 tablespoons ground almonds

Blend the berries, protein powder, yogurt, milk, and ground almonds in a blender until smooth. Makes 2 large glasses.

Discover the delights of frozen fruits and conjure up summer with this berry slushy.

cranberry, raspberry, and vanilla slushy

2 cups cranberry juice
2$^1/_2$ cups frozen raspberries
1 tablespoon superfine sugar
$^3/_4$ cup vanilla yogurt
About 10 ice cubes, crushed

Blend the cranberry juice, frozen raspberries, sugar, yogurt, and ice cubes in a blender until smooth. Makes 2 large glasses.

Note: To make your own vanilla yogurt, simply scrape the seeds from a vanilla bean into a large tub of plain yogurt, add the pod, and refrigerate overnight.

School days were never this cool.

cranberry and vanilla ice-cream soda

3/4 cup cream
1 tablespoon superfine sugar
2 cups cranberry juice
2 cups club soda
4 scoops vanilla ice cream
1/4 cup flaked almonds, toasted

Whip the cream and sugar until soft peaks form. Combine the cranberry juice and club soda. Put a scoop of ice cream into 4 tall glasses. Pour the juice and soda over the ice cream. Spoon the whipped cream over and top with a sprinkling of almonds. Makes 4 medium glasses.

Tangy buttermilk adds protein and oomph to this low-fat fruity smoothie.

plum and prune tang

2 plums, pitted and diced
1 cup prunes, pitted and diced
1 cup low-fat vanilla yogurt
1/2 cup buttermilk
11/4 cups skim milk
8 large ice cubes

Blend the plums, prunes, yogurt, buttermilk, milk, and ice cubes in a blender until smooth. Makes 4 small glasses.

Figs are known as the fruit of love, so serve this up for that someone special.

fig and ginger dream

6 small fresh figs
1-inch x 2-inch piece ginger in syrup, plus 1 teaspoon syrup
2½ cups milk
2 teaspoons natural vanilla extract
Ice cubes, to serve

Blend the figs, ginger, milk, and vanilla in a blender until smooth. Serve over ice. Makes 2 large glasses.

cranberry, raspberry, and vanilla slushy

One a berry, two a berry, three a berry, four.

berry yogurt smoothie

1¹/2 cups strawberries, hulled
1 cup frozen raspberries
1 cup low-fat strawberry yogurt
¹/2 cup cranberry juice

Blend the strawberries, two thirds of the frozen raspberries, the yogurt, and the cranberry juice in a blender until smooth. Serve with a spoon, topped with the remaining raspberries. Makes 4 small glasses.

Too much strawberry is never enough.

summer strawberry smoothie

1 1/2 cups strawberries, hulled
1 cup wildberry drinking yogurt
4 scoops strawberry frozen yogurt
1 tablespoon strawberry sauce
Few drops natural vanilla extract
Ice cubes, to serve

Blend the strawberries, yogurt, frozen yogurt, strawberry sauce, and vanilla in a blender until thick and smooth. Serve over ice. Makes 2 medium glasses.

Serve with buttermilk pancakes for a truly impressive breakfast.

summer buttermilk smoothie

2 peaches
1/3 small cantaloupe (or other orange-fleshed melon), peeled,
    seeded, and chopped
3/4 cup strawberries, hulled
4 mint leaves
1/2 cup buttermilk
1/2 cup orange juice
1 to 2 tablespoons honey

Cut a cross in the base of the peaches. Put them in a heatproof bowl and cover with boiling water. Leave for 1–2 minutes, then remove with a slotted spoon and plunge into cold water. Remove the skin and pits, and slice the flesh. Blend the peaches, cantaloupe, strawberries, and mint leaves in a blender until smooth. Add the buttermilk, orange juice, and 1 tablespoon of the honey and blend to combine. Taste for sweetness and add more honey if needed. Makes 2 medium glasses.

Frozen berries make the grade in all well-stocked freezers.

fruitasia smoothie

2 bananas, chopped
6 strawberries, hulled
3/4 cup frozen raspberries
2 passion fruit
1/3 cup nonfat plain yogurt
1 cup apple juice
2 ice cubes

Blend the bananas, strawberries, frozen raspberries, passion fruit pulp, yogurt, apple juice, and ice cubes in a blender until smooth. Makes 4 small glasses.

summer strawberry smoothie

Use a light, floral honey to avoid overwhelming the delicate
flavor of the custard apple.

custard apple smoothie

2 custard apples, peeled and seeded
2 cups milk
2 teaspoons honey
1 1/2 teaspoons natural vanilla extract
1 teaspoon rose water
Ice cubes, to serve

Blend the custard apple flesh, milk, honey, vanilla, and rose water in a
blender until smooth. Serve over ice. Makes 2 large glasses.

Establish a new tradition at Christmas with this peachy take on an old classic.

peachy eggnog

2 eggs, separated
1/4 cup milk
1/4 cup superfine sugar
1/3 cup cream
13/4 cups peach nectar
2 tablespoons orange juice
Ground nutmeg, to garnish

Beat the egg yolks, milk, and half the sugar in a bowl. Put the bowl over a pan of simmering water—do not allow the base of the bowl to touch the water. Cook, stirring, for 8 minutes, or until the custard thickens. Remove from the heat, cover the surface with plastic wrap, and set aside to cool. Beat the egg whites until frothy. Add the remaining sugar to taste, then beat until stiff peaks form. In a separate bowl, whip the cream until soft peaks form. Gently fold the egg whites and cream into the cooled custard. Stir in the peach nectar and orange juice. Cover and chill for 2 hours. Beat the mixture lightly. Serve sprinkled with nutmeg. Makes 4 small glasses.

Save a glass for the bath and soak your way to silky skin.

apricot and bran breakfast

1/2 cup dried apricots
1 tablespoon oat bran
1/4 cup apricot yogurt
21/2 cups milk
1 tablespoon honey

Soak the dried apricots in boiling water until they are plump and rehydrated, then drain. Blend the apricots, bran, yogurt, milk, and honey in a blender until thick and smooth. Makes 2 large glasses.

Apricots whip up a little potent power pack.

apricot whip

$^1/_3$ cup dried apricots
$^1/_2$ cup apricot yogurt
$^2/_3$ cup light coconut milk
1$^1/_4$ cups milk
1 scoop vanilla ice cream
1 tablespoon honey
Flaked coconut, toasted, to garnish

Soak the dried apricots in boiling water for 15 minutes, then drain and roughly chop. Blend the apricots, yogurt, coconut milk, milk, ice cream, and honey in a blender until smooth. Serve sprinkled with the flaked coconut. Makes 2 medium glasses.

peachy eggnog

Indulge a passion for bananas with this thick shake.

banana passion

3 passion fruit
1 large banana, chopped
¼ cup low-fat plain yogurt
1 cup skim milk

Blend the passion fruit pulp, banana, yogurt, and milk in a blender in short bursts until smooth and the seeds are finely chopped (add more milk if too thick). Don't blend for too long or it will become very bubbly and increase in volume. Makes 2 small glasses.

Sweet, smooth, and a little bit nutty—hmm, sounds like an average day in the office.

banana sesame blend

3 small bananas, chopped
3 cups milk
1½ tablespoons tahini
1½ tablespoons peanut butter
1 tablespoon honey
2 teaspoons natural vanilla extract

Blend the bananas, milk, tahini, peanut butter, honey, and vanilla in a blender until smooth. Makes 2 large glasses.

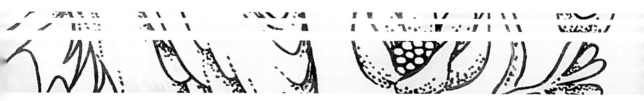

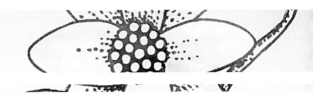

If things have been a little on the turbulent side, save the day with potassium-rich bananas.

banana, kiwifruit, and mint smoothie

2 bananas, chopped
2 kiwifruit, peeled and chopped
1/4 cup mint leaves
1 cup milk or coconut milk
2 scoops vanilla ice cream

Blend the bananas, kiwifruit, mint, milks, and ice cream in a blender until smooth. Makes 2 medium glasses.

Make peace with your sweet tooth and indulge in a standing banana split.

creamy rich banana and macadamia smoothie

2 very ripe bananas, slightly frozen
2/3 cup honey-roasted macadamias
2 tablespoons vanilla honey yogurt
2 cups milk
2 tablespoons wheat germ
1 banana, extra, halved lengthwise

365

Blend the frozen bananas, two-thirds of the macadamias, the yogurt, milk, and wheat germ in a blender for several minutes until thick and creamy. Finely chop the remaining macadamias and put on a plate. Toss the extra banana halves in the nuts to coat. Stand a banana half in each glass or stand on the glass edge. Pour in the smoothie. Makes 2 large glasses.

Note: The bananas need to be very ripe. Peel and chop them, toss in lemon juice, and freeze in an airtight container until ready for use.

creamy rich banana and macadamia smoothie

Get to know your papayas in the best way possible.

papaya and orange smoothie

1 papaya, peeled, seeded, and chopped
1 orange, peeled and chopped
6 to 8 ice cubes
3/4 cup plain yogurt
1 to 2 tablespoons superfine sugar
Ground nutmeg, to serve

Blend the papaya, orange, and ice cubes in a blender until smooth. Add the yogurt and blend to combine. Add the sugar to taste. Serve sprinkled with nutmeg. Makes 2 medium glasses.

Note: This keeps well for 6 hours in the refrigerator. Peach- or apricot-flavored yogurt may be used for added flavor.

Why mess with a classic?

coconut and lime lassi

1 1/2 cups coconut milk
3/4 cup plain yogurt
1/4 cup lime juice
1/4 cup superfine sugar
8 to 10 ice cubes
Lime slices, to garnish

Blend the coconut milk, yogurt, lime juice, sugar, and ice cubes in a blender until well combined and smooth. Serve garnished with lime slices. Makes 2 medium glasses.

Note: Use strong, creamy yogurt to make sure the lassi has tang.

The avocado, master of disguise, is of course a fruit—and one that packs a protein punch.

avocado smoothie

1 small avocado, peeled, pit removed
2 cups milk
3 teaspoons honey
1/2 teaspoon natural vanilla extract

Blend the avocado, milk, honey, and vanilla in a blender until smooth. Makes 2 medium glasses.

Don't judge a book by its cover, this Latin smoothie is a serious heartbreaker.

latin smoothie

1 small avocado, peeled, pit removed
1/2 cup condensed milk
Juice of 1 lime
1 teaspoon natural vanilla extract
8 large ice cubes

Blend the avocado, condensed milk, lime juice, vanilla, ice cubes, and 1 cup water in a blender until smooth. Makes 2 medium glasses.

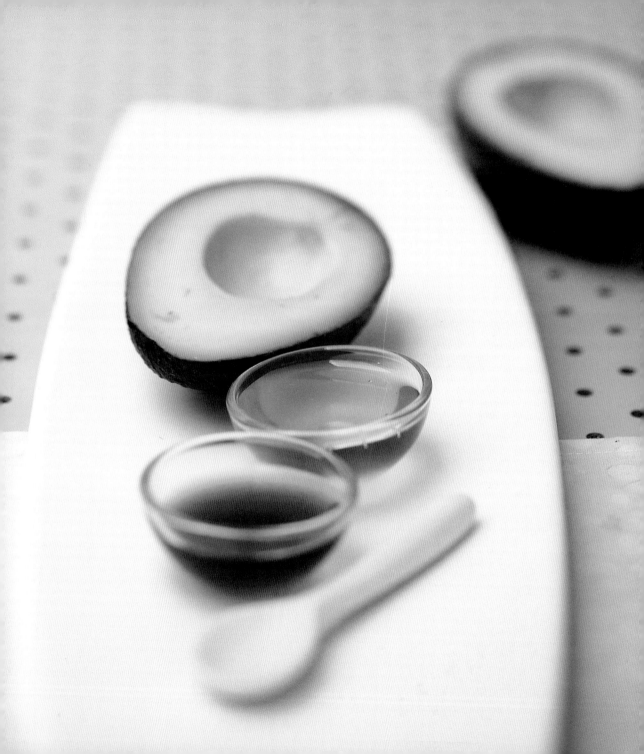

avocado smoothie

Good prepared custard is readily available these days, so feel free to take the easy road to sweetie heaven.

cinnamon and custard shake

1 1/2 cups milk
3/4 cup prepared custard
3 scoops vanilla ice cream
3 teaspoons honey
1 1/2 teaspoons ground cinnamon, plus extra to serve

Blend the milk, custard, ice cream, honey, and cinnamon until smooth and fluffy. Serve sprinkled with extra cinnamon. Makes 2 medium glasses.

A hot, creamy drink at bedtime is one of the few pleasures that lasts a lifetime.

creamy almond and vanilla shake

1 vanilla bean, halved lengthwise
2 cups milk
1/2 cup raw almonds, toasted
1 tablespoon pure maple syrup
1 teaspoon almond extract

Put the vanilla bean and milk into a saucepan and heat until almost boiling. Remove from the heat and set aside to infuse for 5 minutes. Return the pan to the heat and heat again until almost boiling. Remove the vanilla bean. Blend the milk, almonds, maple syrup, and almond extract in a blender until thick and smooth. Makes 2 medium glasses.

Note: You can rinse the vanilla bean, let it dry, and put it in an airtight container of superfine sugar. Use this vanilla sugar to flavor the drink in place of the maple syrup.

Add a plate of shortbread cookies and a bowl of whipped cream for a pared-down take on the real thing.

vanilla apple pie

3 apples, or 1 cup bottled apple juice
1 cup canned apple-pie filling
2 scoops vanilla ice cream
1/2 teaspoon ground cinnamon
1 teaspoon natural vanilla extract
Ground cinnamon or freshly grated nutmeg, to serve, optional

Juice the apples in a juicer. Blend the apple juice, pie filling, ice cream, cinnamon, and vanilla in a blender until smooth. Serve sprinkled with cinnamon or nutmeg, if desired. Makes 2 medium glasses.

Delight your inner child, or even a real one, with this modern take on an old favorite.

apricot crumble smoothie

1 cup canned apricots in natural juice
3/4 cup vanilla yogurt
1 cup milk
1 tablespoon wheat germ
1 tablespoon malted milk powder
Large pinch ground cinnamon

Blend the undrained apricots, yogurt, milk, wheat germ, malted milk powder, and cinnamon in a blender until smooth. Makes 2 large glasses.

Note: Canned peaches, apples, or pears can be used instead of apricots.

apricot crumble smoothie

other ways to be a smoothie Take the road less traveled, the path little beaten, the track grown over with infrequent use. No longer do you need to look longingly at the dairy blends and think, if only

I could—you can! For among coconut and almond milk, tofu and soy milk you have friends stout of heart and firm of flavor. Know truly that dairy milk and its ilk don't necessarily rule the smoothie waves.

A lactose-free option, almond milk is not much thicker than milk, but its flavor is highly distinctive—similar to that of marzipan. It goes well with dates, grapes, peaches, and strawberries and is available from health food stores and Italian delicatessens. Do not buy almond milk syrup, as it is very different. Fresh coconut milk, from whole coconuts, sounds impressive, but let's be honest, the canned variety is a tad easier to find. Coconut cream produces drinks with a better consistency than does coconut milk, but it's higher in fat. With both, buy good-quality brands to ensure milk with a lovely white color. Light coconut milk can also be used; it has a thinner consistency. Blend with tropical fruit, raspberries, and cherries. Silken tofu may seem a strange inclusion here, but its textural qualities and nutritional benefits make it a welcome one. Its smoothie partners are tropical fruits such as bananas and mangoes. Unlike cow milk or goat milk, soy milk does not contain lactose sugar or cholesterol. It has antioxidant benefits but little calcium, so buy calcium-fortified soy milk if you're using it in place of dairy products. Soy milk can be quite sweet, so taste before adding other sweeteners. Use with warm flavors such as pears, cinnamon, dates, and apricots. Soy yogurt and soy ice cream are also good choices. Extras: carob powder is sweet and has a similar flavor to chocolate but without the fat. Lecithin meal is a natural soy-derived nutritional supplement. Its reputed properties range from aiding the liver to improving memory. Buy both from health food stores.

Smooth, thick, and calming, consider using any leftovers as a fragrant facial!

almond, papaya, and date shake

1/2 papaya, peeled, seeded, and chopped
4 fresh dates, pitted and chopped
11/2 cups almond milk
1 teaspoon rose water
Ice cubes, to serve

Blend the papaya, dates, almond milk, and rose water in a blender until smooth. Serve over ice. Makes 2 medium glasses.

Almond milk is special-occasion material in the Middle East,
but don't let that stop you from making this often.

almond and grape frappé

2³/4 cups green seedless grapes
1 cup almond milk
Large pinch ground cinnamon
8 large ice cubes

Juice the grapes in a juicer. Blend the grape juice, almond milk, cinnamon, and ice cubes in a blender until smooth. Makes 2 medium glasses.

Note: Almonds are high in calcium and an excellent inclusion in a dairy-free diet.

A veritable bazaar of flavors—sweet, nutty, and smooth as a bolt of silk.

whipped nougat

1 cup canned apricots in natural juice
2 cups almond milk
1½ teaspoons natural vanilla extract
1 teaspoon honey
Few drops rose water, optional
8 large ice cubes

Blend the undrained apricots, almond milk, vanilla, honey, rose water, and ice cubes in a blender until smooth. Makes 2 large glasses.

Cherries seem so indulgent—this drink will do nothing to change that impression.

almond cherry smoothie

1 1/2 cups almond milk
2 cups cherries, pitted
1/4 teaspoon natural vanilla extract
Pinch ground cinnamon
4 large ice cubes

Blend the almond milk, cherries, vanilla, cinnamon, and ice cubes in a blender until smooth. Makes 2 large glasses.

Note: If you like a strong almond or marzipan flavor, add a dash of almond extract.

almond cherry smoothie

This one takes us back to our trampoline days (without having to do the actual bouncing).

coconut milk and raspberry shake

2¹/2 cups raspberries
1 cup apple and black currant juice
1¹/2 cups coconut milk
2 scoops vanilla soy ice cream
Marshmallows, to serve

Blend the raspberries, apple and black currant juice, coconut milk, and ice cream in a blender for several minutes until thick and creamy. Thread marshmallows onto 4 swizzle sticks and serve with the shakes, along with a straw and a long spoon. Makes 4 small glasses.

Note: For a low-fat drink, blend the raspberries and juice with ice instead of coconut milk and ice cream.

Okay, so this is not one for the dieters, but that's just the way it is sometimes.

cherrycoco

2 cups cherries, pitted
1¹/₂ cups coconut milk
2 teaspoons superfine sugar
1 teaspoon natural vanilla extract
Ice cubes, to serve

Juice the cherries in a juicer. Shake well with the coconut milk, sugar, and vanilla. Serve over ice. Makes 2 small glasses.

Note: You could use vanilla sugar in this recipe—just keep a vanilla bean in a jar of sugar for fragrant sugar.

Papa don't preach, I'm taking good care of myself with a healthy dose of papaya.

coconut and papaya frappé

1/2 papaya, peeled, seeded, and chopped
11/2 cups coconut milk
2 tablespoons lime juice
2 tablespoons superfine sugar
1 teaspoon natural vanilla extract
Pinch allspice
8 large ice cubes

Blend the papaya, coconut milk, lime juice, sugar, vanilla, allspice, and ice cubes in a blender until smooth. Makes 2 large glasses.

I've got a lovely bunch of coconuts, so let's make some ice, ice, baby.

coconut and lime ice

1¹/₂ cups coconut milk
Juice of 4 limes
2 teaspoons natural vanilla extract
¹/₃ cup superfine sugar
¹/₃ cup mint leaves, optional
8 large ice cubes

Blend the coconut milk, lime juice, vanilla, sugar, mint, and ice cubes in a blender until smooth. Makes 2 large glasses.

coconut milk and raspberry shake

When the island breeze is calling but work has you stalling,

take an instant vacation with this tropical shake.

coconut and mango shake

1 1/2 cups fresh mango pulp
1/2 cup lime juice
1/2 cup coconut milk
2 teaspoons honey
3 teaspoons finely chopped mint
12 large ice cubes

Blend the mango pulp, lime juice, coconut milk, honey, mint, and ice cubes in a blender until thick and smooth. Chill well. Stir to combine. Makes 2 medium glasses.

Go the whole hog and serve this in cocktail glasses with lychees on toothpicks. And perhaps a splash of white rum.

pineapple and lychee creamy colada

1/3 pineapple, peeled and chopped
3 cups pineapple juice
2 2/3 cups canned lychees
2 tablespoons spearmint leaves
1/2 cup coconut milk
Crushed ice

Blend the pineapple, pineapple juice, lychees and their juice, and spearmint in a blender until smooth. Add the coconut milk and crushed ice and blend until thick and smooth. Makes 6 medium glasses.

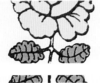

If you've been good, reward yourself by using coconut milk for an extra-luscious treat.

island blend

1/3 pineapple, peeled and chopped
1/2 small papaya, peeled, seeded, and chopped
2 small bananas, chopped
1/4 cup coconut milk
1 cup orange juice
Ice cubes, to serve

Blend the pineapple, papaya, bananas, and coconut milk in a blender until smooth. Add the orange juice and blend until combined. Serve over ice. Makes 2 medium glasses.

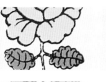

For a kitsch centerpiece, serve this in a hollowed-out pineapple.

coconut and pineapple iced drink

1 pineapple, peeled
1 cup coconut milk
Mint leaves, to garnish
Pineapple leaves, to garnish

399

Juice the pineapple in a juicer and pour the juice into a large pitcher. Stir in the coconut milk. Pour 1/2 cup of the mixture into 8 holes of an ice-cube tray and freeze. Chill the remaining mixture. When the ice cubes have frozen, pour the juice mixture into 2 glasses, add the ice cubes, and garnish with mint and pineapple leaves. Makes 2 medium glasses.

pineapple and lychee creamy colada

Ascend to berry yogurt heaven with a clear conscience.

strawberry lassi

1¹/2 cups strawberries, hulled
1¹/4 cups strawberry soy yogurt
2 tablespoons honey
4 ice cubes

Blend the strawberries, yogurt, honey, ice cubes, and 2¹/2 tablespoons water in a blender until smooth. Garnish with any leftover strawberries. Makes 2 small glasses.

This drink is musky and full of promise, with gentle warmth.

spiced melon shake

1/4 teaspoon cardamom seeds
1 1/3 cups creamy soy milk
1/2 cantaloupe (or other orange-fleshed melon), peeled, seeded,
    and chopped
1 tablespoon honey
2 tablespoons ground almonds
4 ice cubes

Lightly crush the cardamom seeds in a mortar and pestle or with the back
of a knife. Blend the cardamom and soy milk in a blender for 30 seconds.
Strain the soy milk and rinse any remaining seeds from the blender. Return
the strained milk to the blender, add the cantaloupe, honey, almonds, and
ice cubes, and blend until smooth. Makes 2 medium glasses.

Buy these summer fruits by the tray and develop a smoothie habit you won't need to kick.

apricot tofu smoothie

4 apricots, pits removed
2 peaches, pits removed
1 cup apricot nectar
2/3 cup silken tofu

Blend the apricots, peaches, apricot nectar, and tofu in a blender until smooth. Makes 2 medium glasses.

No corny jokes about soy good for you—one mouthful and you'll know it's true.

fresh date and pear soy shake

1 1/2 cups creamy soy milk
4 fresh dates, pitted and chopped
2 small pears, peeled, cored and chopped

Blend the soy milk, dates, and pears in a blender until smooth. Makes 2 medium glasses.

strawberry lassi

Not a roadside attraction, just an ideal way to start the day.

big bold banana

3 cups soy milk
1/2 cup silken tofu
4 very ripe bananas, chopped
1 tablespoon honey
1 tablespoon natural vanilla extract
1 tablespoon carob powder (see Note)

Blend the soy milk, tofu, bananas, honey, vanilla, and carob powder in a blender until smooth. Serve with long spoons. Makes 4 medium glasses.

Note: Carob powder is available from health food stores.

Coffee and breakfast in one easy package.

banana soy latte

1³⁄4 cups coffee-flavored soy milk
2 bananas, chopped
8 large ice cubes
1 teaspoon powdered drinking chocolate
1⁄4 teaspoon ground cinnamon

Blend the soy milk and bananas in a blender until smooth. With the blender running, add the ice cubes one at a time until well incorporated. Serve sprinkled with the drinking chocolate and ground cinnamon. Makes 4 small glasses.

If the aloha evening breeze swept you away, rest and repair the morning after.

tropical morning soy smoothie

2 mangoes, chopped
1 1/3 cups creamy soy milk
2/3 cup pineapple juice
1/4 cup chopped mint
6 ice cubes
Mint sprigs, to garnish

Blend the mango, soy milk, pineapple juice, mint, and ice cubes in a blender until smooth. Serve garnished with mint. Makes 2 large glasses.

Keep Mom happy and make this breakfast-in-a-glass part of your routine.

get-up-and-go smoothie

1/2 mango, chopped
1/4 cup vanilla soy yogurt
2 cups nonfat soy milk
2 tablespoons oat bran
2 tablespoons honey

411

Blend the mango, yogurt, soy milk, oat bran, and honey in a blender until smooth. Serve with spoons. Makes 4 small glasses.

banana soy latte

Breakfast is the most important meal of the day, but there is no reason why it shouldn't also be the yummiest.

maple banana breakfast

1 1/3 cups fresh or creamy soy milk
2/3 cup vanilla soy yogurt
2 very ripe bananas, chopped
1 large yellow peach, chopped
2 teaspoons lecithin meal
2 tablespoons maple syrup

Blend the soy milk, yogurt, bananas, peach, lecithin meal, and maple syrup in a blender until smooth. Makes 2 medium glasses.

Fill a thermos for an emergency breakfast on the run that really works.

wheaty starter

1 cup wheat breakfast cereal
2 bananas, chopped
¼ cup vanilla soy yogurt
2 cups nonfat soy milk

Blend the cereal, bananas, yogurt, and soy milk in a blender until smooth. Makes 4 small glasses.

Don't throw away black, spotted bananas, their lush ripeness is the highlight of this smoothie.

carob peanut smoothie

1 1/2 cups carob- or chocolate-flavored soy milk
2 very ripe bananas, chopped
2/3 cup silken tofu
2 tablespoons honey
1 tablespoon peanut butter

Blend the soy milk, bananas, tofu, honey, and peanut butter in a blender until smooth. Makes 2 medium or 4 small glasses.

Strong, sweet, and powerful—a real superhero!

peanut choc power smoothie

2 cups chocolate-flavored soy milk
1/2 cup silken tofu
1/4 cup peanut butter
2 bananas, chopped
2 tablespoons chocolate syrup
8 large ice cubes

Blend the soy milk, tofu, peanut butter, bananas, chocolate syrup, and ice cubes in a blender until smooth. Makes 4 small glasses.

carob peanut smoothie

index

423

424

425

426

427

428

429

430

431